S0-ANE-931

THE 90% RULE
What's your next big opportunity?

HOW ENTREPRENEURIAL THINKING CAN INSPIRE INNOVATIVE
AND SUSTAINABLE GROWTH IN YOUR ORGANIZATION.

THE 90% RULE
What's your next big opportunity?

HOW ENTREPRENEURIAL THINKING CAN INSPIRE INNOVATIVE
AND SUSTAINABLE GROWTH IN YOUR ORGANIZATION.

by

Ken Tencer

and

John Paulo Cardoso

Spyder*works*®

NEW YORK | TORONTO

All rights reserved.

No part of this publication may be reproduced or transmitted in any form or by any means, electronic or mechanical, including photocopy, recording, or any information storage and retrieval system, without permission in writing from Spyder Works Inc.

Requests for permission to make copies of any part of the work should be directed to Spyder Works Inc. or, in the case of material reproduced here from elsewhere, to the original copyright holder.

Information on how to obtain copies of this book is available at:
Web site: http://www.90percentrule.com
E-mail: info@90percentrule.com
Telephone: 877.281.7896
Fax: 905.608.9480

ISBN 1450513549

Every reasonable effort has been made to acquire permission for copyrighted materials used in this book and to acknowledge such permissions accurately. Any errors or omissions called to Spyder Works Inc. attention will be corrected in future printings.

Printed in USA.

Dedicated to those who "Leap and grow wings as they fall."

Table of Contents

PART III: The Next 10%

Preface

By Rick Spence

*President, Canadian Entrepreneur
Communications, National Entrepreneurship
Columnist,* National Post, *Former editor and
publisher,* PROFIT Magazine

It's the toughest challenge in business: to come up with consistent innovations that allow you to keep pace with (or preferably anticipate) your customers' changing needs. And to do so without breaking the bank, or putting the company at risk by galloping in many directions at once.

In my years as editor of PROFIT, *The Magazine for Canadian Entrepreneurs*, I saw a few companies that pulled off this kind of ongoing innovation—and many more that failed. Research In Motion, Gap Adventures, McCain Foods, Cirque du Soleil, Spin Master Ltd. and yes, Google, are some of the celebrated companies that have solved the problem of what I called "strategic diversification" growing on multiple fronts, through continuing product and service innovation, with minimal deviations from the core strategy. These are companies that don't bet it all on one "big win" but on lots of little wins instead.

From personal pager to always-on email device (RIM). From one show in Montreal to 20 around the world—including seven in Vegas alone (Cirque). From french fries to frozen pizza to dim sum (McCain). Winning companies take what they know and leverage that knowledge to challenge new markets—building on strength rather than random chance.

The essence of strategic diversification is to venture into the unknown—but only a little way. A safe distance into the dark, flashlight (and spare battery) in hand. Never to get in so deep that you endanger what you've already accomplished. And never to go so far that you can't find your way back. Sounds simple but it's really not. Because you're asking entrepreneurs to pursue their dreams—systematically; with patience and discipline. It's like telling your teenager to be home by nine-thirty.

In this book, the strategists of Spyder Works draw on their skills and years of client experience to create a step-by-step guide to strategic diversification based on what Ken Tencer and John Paulo Cardoso call *The 90% Rule™*. I believe their dynamic but doable approach can revolutionize business by taking the pain, uncertainty and risk out of expansion. Drawing on examples from their own business, from clients and from global market leaders such as Gap Adventures, Apple and Pepsi, they have synthesized successful growth strategies in to a series of practical exercises that will help businesses understand their strengths, sort good opportunities from bad and leap boldly (but never rashly) into new markets.

Again, some of this sounds much easier to do than it is. For one thing, Ken and John insist that companies need to understand who they are and what they do best before moving into new products and markets. Few stick to this. I have interviewed a few thousand companies and CEOs in more than 25 years as a business journalist, and in my experience, few organizations do this because they really don't understand their core competencies—the unique combination of assets, intelligence and talent that provide their competitive advantage. If you don't know what you do best, how can you possibly decide what is best to do next? And therein lies the reason so many new products and growth strategies fail.

You need to give your business every chance to succeed. After all, success is hard. Winning once doesn't mean you can do it again. In fact, it may be setting you up for future failure. Only rigorous self-examination and systematic market analysis can reliably bring

I believe their dynamic but doable approach can revolutionize business by taking the pain, uncertainty and risk out of expansion.

you to victory, and even then, frankly, your chances are 50-50 at best. Business is a complex beast, markets are always in motion and success can never be guaranteed (cue the Apple Newton).

And yet, opportunity abounds. The world has never been so hungry for new products and services or in greater need of innovative solutions. The growing niches of consumers demanding more and better products, a time-starved middle class demanding more personal and timely services, emerging middle and upper-class populations around the globe, and business markets facing increasing competition and growing technological challenges all define marketplaces that are robust, motivated and needful of the new. The rewards are there for innovative entrepreneurs and organizations who figure out how to tap these new markets with minimal risk.

Whether you work for a small business or a multinational corporation, you and your colleagues need a jolt of entrepreneurial thinking. And that doesn't mean running around chasing every shiny object you see. At its best, entrepreneurial thinking entails two parts: First, being aware of all the opportunities around you; and secondly, remaining committed to exploring these opportunities in a focused, disciplined way—never venturing too far into the unknown. It's akin to the old adage that the best entrepreneurs aren't risk-takers: they're risk-avoiders. If they're going to put their own money and personal reputations on the line, they had better do so with care and caution, soberly setting their objectives, painstakingly researching the markets, and double-checking their tactics. Entrepreneurial thinking is about doing the very best job you can with what you have and not accepting those limited resources as a licence to practice the cowboy capitalism of "ready, fire, aim."

As Ken and John say; it's about evolution, not revolution.

It's about evolution, not revolution.

In this book, your authors clearly explain what entrepreneurial thinking means. Know what you're good at. Learn how to communicate that strategic message clearly and consistently, to make sure everyone on the team understands where they're going. Build strong, intimate relationships with your customers; know their needs as well as you do your own. Cultivate innovative thinking that emphasizes how you can help your customers satisfy those needs, now and in the future. Map and compare competing opportunities and then reinvent your business to serve the most promising "contiguous" niches. Involve your key team members throughout this process and create metrics that will engage them and make sure the work gets done according to the pace you set. All these steps are in this book.

Here's how to make the most of it: Read through the book quickly getting to the end as soon as you can, so you understand the process it encompasses and the results that can accrue. Won't take you long. Then go through it again, more carefully this time, making sure that you and your team actually carry out the exercises that you judge most valuable. This is not just a book to be read: it is a toolkit, with information and insights you need to share directly with your team and directions for you and your colleagues to follow.

Don't begrudge the time it takes to do these exercises and think things out as prescribed: this kind of creative collaboration is the foundation of business success. The advice in this book outlines a series of "best practices" that can't help but result in a smarter, more focused customer-facing organization. All this work is an essential investment in future success, not just another distraction from the day-to-day routine.

The ideas and processes described in this book are strategic differentiators that will help you stand out in your industry and grow with the most promising niches in your market. But only if you lift them off the printed page and set them free throughout your organization to influence the way you think, speak, plan and do business.

I have spent a lot of time exploring what may be the entrepreneur's biggest weakness: the reluctance to actually do the work they know needs to be done. Given their choice, some would rather clean out the office toilet than revise their business plan. Others would rather fiddle with product specs or sales commissions rather than launch a series of staff-customer consultations to find out exactly what their clients think of them and where they are headed next. Of course, most of us would rather do the things that are easy than things that are hard. This "entrepreneurial inertia" dooms organizations to subpar performance. So use your competitors' inertia to your own advantage. Be the one reader in 100 that actually asks the questions suggested in this book, works through these exercises and discovers the powerful strategic insights that are waiting for you. Embody the change you wish to see.

Success is more than luck or timing. Success is a disciplined approach to creating results. With a methodology such as *The 90% Rule*™, you can now shift the odds in your favor.

You deserve no less. Go for it!

Rick Spence

Part
One

Chapter 1

Forward

I found a way.

Entrepreneur's credo

No, I didn't spell foreword wrong. This isn't a preface, you've already read that. This is a direction and a directive—a call to action—for those who want to get more out of their business. More growth for less financial investment. In a word: leverage.

If you are one of those people who get out of bed every morning to make a difference, then your entrepreneurial spirit and thinking are alive and well. And if your energy is rooted in audacity, you're ahead of the game. To some, audacity may be a negative concept, associated with an attitude or edge, but the real definition centers on the *willingness to challenge assumptions and conventions.* Without audacity and an entrepreneurial mindset, we'd be short many of today's taken-for-granted conveniences, such as the printing press, boats, trains, cars, planes, phones, radios, computers, BlackBerries, iPods, FedEx, Google, Twitter, etc.

Let me be clear, this book is not intended to make everyone an entrepreneur. This book tells you how to use

No, I didn't spell foreword wrong. This isn't a preface, you've already read that. This is a direction and a directive—a call to action—for those who want to get more out of their business.

entrepreneurial thinking, attitude and action to leverage the assets you already have. Because at the core of the *90% Rule* is entrepreneurial thinking, which steadfastly believes that there is never a shortage of opportunities, only a perceived shortage of resources to capitalize on them. Problem is, there are two all too common challenges:

- First, companies have limited capital available so there is always a lack of resources (time, people, money) to develop the best opportunities. And too many people see that as a roadblock instead of a call to action.
- Secondly, many companies chase opportunities on a tactical basis, rather than strategically because they have not defined the broader context in which they are making decisions.

The 90% Rule™ allows you to successfully overcome these common impediments by addressing five fundamentals:

1. Gain maximum leverage with the assets you already have
2. Understand your core business from a visionary level
3. Identify and profile your most lucrative target markets
4. Develop logical, next-step projects that are actionable and measurable—and *in keeping with* your vision and strategy
5. Make innovation a front-burner issue so that you are always a step ahead of your competitors and the market.

Entrepreneurs are simply those who understand that there is little difference between obstacle and opportunity and are able to turn both to their advantage.

Victor Kiam, former CEO, Remington Corporation

Entrepreneurial thinking: Achieving more with less

Let me first mention two common examples that are the antithesis of entrepreneurial thinking. For years I've heard "news" stories where a CEO announces that his or her company will shed non-core assets and focus on doing what it does best. I would ask, "Why did you get away from your core business in the first place?" A good entrepreneur never loses sight of this. Secondly, too often I have heard traditional consultants go into successful, profitable companies and tell them what's *wrong* with the business instead of building on what's *right*. It makes no sense to me and is not the way an entrepreneurial mind works.

Entrepreneurs have always fascinated me. I've studied them for years in order to better understand how they think. The great ones, from Gutenberg to Ford to Branson have a knack for seeing the big opportunities and finding a way to make them happen no matter what the odds. This is the essence of entrepreneurial thinking.

I believe that entrepreneurial thinking is at the root of all successful change, innovation and growth. And the good news is that everyone can cultivate their own entrepreneurial thinking to help change their business and improve their professional and personal growth.

By entrepreneurial thinking I mean the ability to envision and think about opportunities at many different levels; to see both the big picture and the relevant details within the big picture; to act on those details in the most innovative way possible; and to do it with limited resources. Entrepreneurial thinking is creative, innovative and resourceful thought, anchored in the power of leverage, in order to get the most out of the resources you already have—the *90% Rule*™.

By entrepreneurial thinking I mean the ability to envision and think about opportunities at many different levels; to see both the big picture and the relevant details within the big picture; to act on those details in the most innovative way possible; and to do it with limited resources.

The *90% Rule* focuses on expanding the individual and collective capacity for entrepreneurial thinking in order to accelerate innovation and growth. It is an organizing principle designed around a process that cultivates the inherent entrepreneurial thinking in an organization in order to convert its best opportunities into innovative new action and leverage core assets into sustainable growth.

Our seminars and this book—and all our thinking and action—are instilled with the spirit of entrepreneurial thinking because that is the driving force behind any successful business (regardless of size). Most importantly, entrepreneurial thinking fuels passion, will, innovation, and an organization's most fundamental tool, leverage. But the thinking alone is not enough; it needs a means to reach its end, a way of converting its power into actionable, measurable, profitable opportunities.

Three "how tos"

One of the objectives of this book is to help you continuously improve your business by imbedding three things:

1) How to foster continuous innovation and growth through the doctrine of entrepreneurial thinking—"innovation against all odds"—by leveraging intellectual and customer capital, continually generating ideas and opportunities and executing it all without bundles of additional money.

2) How to develop a disciplined process that builds on and reinforces, the best in your organization, people, products and services. And through the principles of entrepreneurial thinking, elevates everything to new levels.

3) How to install and implement a systematic and iterative process that pursues opportunities that you are already 90% capable of achieving.

Six applications of *The 90% Rule*™

There are many different types of organizations that can benefit from the application of the *90% Rule* and I have indicated below a half-dozen general categories.

1. Focus a new management team (or re-focus an existing one):
When an organization needs a cohesive new focus around a new management team and/or new initiatives, the *90% Rule* uncovers and then shines a spotlight on the highest potential opportunities.

2. Preparing for a funding initiative:
When funding is needed, the *90% Rule* can help you to identify the critical strategic and tactical elements and the requisite leverage that a lender is looking for.

3. Family business in transition:
When a family business is transitioning to the next generation, the *90% Rule* can help families keep the business goals and overall vision in focus—and detrimental change to a minimum.

4. Sales have hit a plateau:
When organizational culture and brands are stagnated and need new insights and greater innovation, the *90% Rule* can lead you to some very high-value returns.

5. More opportunities than resources:
When there are more opportunities to pursue than resources to support them, the *90% Rule* helps prioritize and manage resource allocation.

6. Shifts in markets and customer needs:
When markets are shifting or customers' needs and wants are experiencing incessant change, the *90% Rule* can help you identify and prioritize the best opportunities on an ongoing basis.

Whether or not your organization's challenges fall neatly into one of the above categories, I can assure you that the *90% Rule* applies in almost every situation because it is rooted in the fundamental principle of leverage. Keep in mind, one of its strengths is based on the fact that you are already 90% of the way there.

> **The entrepreneur is the most important player in the building of the global economy.**
> **So much so that big companies are decentralizing and reconstituting themselves as networks of entrepreneurs.**
>
> *John Naisbitt, author Global Paradox and Megatrends*

Apple: Entrepreneurial thinking at its best

It may be the world's most successful turnaround. By the late 1990's, Apple Computer was swimming in a sea of red ink, its glory days as a disruptive innovator in the personal computer industry now long behind it. Microsoft's Windows programs had appropriated the graphical, easy-to-use operating system that had made Apple's Macintosh so popular among artists, designers and engineers. Microsoft's unmatched distribution power was slowly crushing Apple's innovation edge.

Apple's co-founder, Steve Jobs, had returned to the company after a decade away, receiving a rare second chance to work his design magic. While Jobs introduced such innovations as the rounded, one-piece iMac computer (processor and monitor in one desktop unit!), Apple continued to lose market share.

But Jobs, who had also dabbled in computer animation after investing in Pixar (producer of *Toy Story*) during his years away from Apple, had another plan up his sleeve. Apple didn't have to confine its high-end design skills and usability expertise to the PC market. Technology was now transforming consumer culture—not just in animation, but now particularly in music, where convergence of computer and communications technology had suddenly created a huge market for portable music (and illegal copying of songs over the Internet, through file-sharing sites such as Napster).

Combining Apple's hardware expertise with Jobs' insistence on leading-edge design, in October 2001 Apple introduced the iPod: a gleaming white piece of plastic with an intuitive scroll-wheel interface that could store and replay 1,000 songs. Although not the first MP3 player, the petite but powerful iPod was the first to make the category sexy and Apple's distinctive "ear buds" became a sought-after status symbol.

With its engineering horsepower, Apple regularly turned out innovative new iPod models, beefing up their storage capacity even as the product shrunk to make it more convenient and almost weightless. By 2006, the iPod accounted for nearly half of Apple's revenues.

Jobs also addressed the problem of music piracy. Using Apple's 75% share in portable music players he created iTunes: a centralized, easy-to-use system for managing music that later proved so powerful that Jobs was able to force the recording industry to accept his take-it-or-leave-it price of just 99 cents a song. iTunes has now sold more than two billion songs.

The rest is history. In 2007 Apple's iPhone transformed the market, combining Apple's computer expertise, Internet experience and user knowledge. Now the iPhone has led to a new level of Apple-based innovation, as more than 100,000 software developers, worldwide, create new iPhone applications for downloading through Apple's "App Store."

With sales of $32 billion in 2008 (six times the revenue of 2002), Apple has proved that a core competency in one industry can be carried into other markets. For its next act, Jobs intends to revolutionize the video experience through Apple TV. "We're making our most innovative products ever," he said triumphantly in mid-2009, "and our customers are responding."

Even as a large company, Apple thinks and acts like a small, agile, ever-changing organization, driven by entrepreneurial thinking.

Entrepreneurial thinking is inherent in every organization, it simply needs to be tapped and converted, everyday, by everybody.

— *Tencer and Cardoso*

The 90% Rule™

Getting more out of what you already have and do

Innovation is the specific instrument of entrepreneurship ... the act that endows resources with new capacity to create wealth.

Peter Drucker, American management consultant and author

I selected Peter Drucker's quotation because it touches on three important components of the *90% Rule*—innovation, entrepreneurship and new capacity. The first two, when combined with a systematic method of prioritization, will give you the objective "new capacity to create wealth." The best part is, you just have to change some of your thinking—actually, cultivate a new way of thinking—and use it to better leverage what you already have.

When I read *Outliers: The Story of Success* by Malcolm Gladwell, I was struck by a quote and its relation to the *90% Rule*. Neurologist Daniel Levitin writes, "The emerging picture from such studies is that ten thousand hours of practice is required to achieve the level of mastery associated with

To my way of thinking, it makes no sense to try and become an expert in a whole new field or new market when your next big opportunity probably lies in a simple extension of your current business, brand or mastery.

being a world-class expert—in anything."[1] To Gladwell, this is the recipe for outstanding success in any field. On the other hand, it's also a useful reminder of the inherent difficulties in trying to excel in too many fields.

To my way of thinking, it makes no sense to try and become an expert in a whole new field or new market when your next big opportunity probably lies in a simple extension of your current business, brand or mastery. It's about figuring out how what you do fits better in current markets or in adjacent markets or vertical businesses. Based on Levitin's calculation, the *90% Rule* already puts you nine thousand hours ahead and on the way to being an expert in your next big opportunity. So extend and build on your current capital base; don't over-leverage to acquire a new one.

The Power of the *90% Rule*: More with less

Application of the *90% Rule* uncovers the greatest opportunities for growth and success based on what your organization is already 90% capable of doing. It gets you to capitalize on, and leverage, your existing resources such as time, money, intellectual capital, customer capital, product capital, brand equity and physical assets. You may be surprised at your existing capacity to generate *more* with *less*.

You are 90% there

The *90% Rule* is akin to an essay that philosopher Isaiah Berlin, *The Hedgehog and the Fox*[2] , borrowed from a similar ancient Greek parable. It's about slow and sure rather than fast and risky—evolution, not revolution. The story divides the world into hedgehogs and foxes. The fox knows many things and pursues many things, but the hedgehog knows one big thing and pursues it relentlessly. Hedgehogs simplify a complex world into one single powerful organizing idea,

[1] *Outliers: The Story of Success* by Malcolm Gladwell, page 40

a basic principle or concept that unifies and guides everything it knows, thinks and does. The *90% Rule* is like the hedgehog, a principle designed to enable you to build and sustain new capacity and create wealth on your existing base.

Do the math: Why do we only embrace the power of compound interest in our personal investments?

The principle and the beauty of the *90% Rule* can be seen in this mathematical example.

Define your prior year's sales as your core sales. Set these core sales as 90% of the next year's sales. If this core 90% of your business grows at 5% a year, then that generates 4.5% annual growth. Now, add a new product, service, store or vertical that expands your sales base by an additional 10%. Result: you will achieve annual growth of 14.5%. If you can continue this incremental growth strategy, your business will double in size in about five years. Just as important, that growth will require only a moderate investment in terms of financing, staffing and operations. Your business can make a big impact with small, logical, manageable next steps.

Operating leverage as a marketing tool™

I am a big believer in using *Operating leverage as a marketing tool* ™ , which is a cornerstone of the *90% Rule*. This is quite different than a strict belief in the traditional definition of operating leverage.

Traditionally, operating leverage is the reliance on, or investment in, fixed assets. We all know it's necessary to understand your monthly overhead but it makes little difference if you have too many fixed assets, because then you are constantly scrambling to cover costs every month. Traditional financial leverage is the reliance on debt to fund growth and increase production. But too much debt or too

[2] Isaiah Berlin, *The Hedgehog and the Fox,* an essay, *The Study of Mankind,* p.436

Why do we only embrace the power of compound interest in our personal investments?

many fixed assets (coupled with a dip in sales) and, well, your banker is your new, not-so-best friend. The need is to strike a reasonable balance so that when the unexpected happens— quite expectedly—you can survive it. But it's not about disproportionate borrowing or investing.

Obviously, both points of leverage are inherent in almost any business. You will always have some fixed assets and bank borrowing is a fact of life for most of us. But, and it's a big but, there is a better way to view leverage in your business.

We haven't got the money, so we've got to think.

Ernest Rutherford, British physicist

Untapped leverage

Good leverage gets the most out of your current strengths, which is where the critical focus must be. Focus on what's right, not what's wrong. Dealing from strength.

It's about rethinking and reunderstanding the business you are in and the capital investments you have already made (e.g., intellectual capital), as well as the ways in which your business serves its customers and potential customers (e.g., customer capital).

I was recently at a business luncheon and the keynote speaker was talking about how they had rethought their business, both internally and with the input of their customers. Through the process, they began to understand that they were not specifically in the hearing aid business but, what I will call, the hearing device technology business. They were leaders at assisting people to hear things more clearly while blocking out external noise. This revelation enabled them to leverage their existing expertise by applying their hearing device technology to emerging markets like blue tooth ear pieces for cell phones and military applications.

This type of thinking is using operating leverage as a marketing tool versus traditional financial leverage. This is the principle of *getting more out of what you already have.*

Harley-Davidson dealership

When Wilmington, Delaware entrepreneur Mike Schwartz bought himself a run-down Harley-Davidson dealership in 1994, he believed he could boost revenues and profits by modernizing some of its dated sales and management processes. He didn't dream that by going to the root of what makes Harley one of the world's most-loved brands, he would turn that five employee business into a $100-million shrine to "the American Road."

After founding two successful businesses, in cell phones and sports tickets, Schwartz, at the age of 32, was just looking to relax when he bought his first Harley Softail cruiser in 1992. But he soon fell in love with the romantic-outlaw mystique of Harleys and bought the local dealership for $325,000. By fixing the leaky roof, professionalizing the sales process and creating a more customer-friendly environment, he turned the business around. Four years later, when a larger lot came vacant in nearby New Castle, just off Interstate 295, Schwartz decided to build the dealership of his dreams.

Mike's Famous Harley-Davidson is now much more than a dealership; it's a monument to the American dream, the open road, freedom and the wind on your face. Schwartz brought the Harley brand to life by surrounding his dealership with a roadhouse restaurant ("best chili in the state") and a museum dedicated to Harleys, American road trips, and old motels and gas stations. Of course, he sells Harley leather jackets, accessories and collectibles for riders and sidewalk spectators alike. And even the chrome-filled showroom was designed to look like an antique (though spotlessly clean) warehouse.

Today his 40,000 square-foot-complex is as much a tourist destination as a bike store, servicing and selling the 100% American-made "Hogs" as well as the dreams that go with them. "I decided to make buying a Harley a one-of-a-kind experience the buyer wouldn't soon forget," says Schwartz. "My place is rough and solid, like a Harley. It delivers great emotion and the great American past." He says he isn't really selling motorcycles; he's selling fun (although no one is allowed to forget the solemn purpose of the business – a gong is struck every time a new motorcycle is sold).

By reinventing his business as a family attraction, Schwartz overcame the tattoo-wearing, bad-biker stigma still attached to some Harley dealerships. And he's never looked back. Today, Mike's Famous is the largest Harley dealer in the United States. Mike himself owns four Harley dealerships as well as two other power sports dealers specializing in motorcycles, ATVs and jet skis.

Throughout the book, I will include examples of companies that exemplify the *90% Rule*.

Different lens, different view

We all know how important it is to understand current and potential customers, to know the core competencies of our businesses and to be aware of what new products, adjacent markets and services we are already 90% capable of providing. But most companies get stuck in the everyday rut of trying to meet operational efficiencies, productivity and throughput. As a result, they always see their operations through the same set of lenses based on the same assumptions; consequently, they get the same results. Think back to the hearing aid company that morphed to hearing device technology. If they hadn't rethought (or relensed) their business they might have missed out on one of the largest opportunities ever, the market for cell phone ear pieces, driven by the government legislation making these the only legal way to use a cell phone while driving.

I was to learn later in life that we tend to meet any new situation by reorganizing; and a wonderful method it can be for creating the illusion of progress while producing confusion, inefficiency and demoralization.

Gaius Petronius Arbiter, 66 A.D.

This is not about "reorganizing," rather it is about relooking, rethinking, redoing. It's looking at strategic opportunities through a new set of lenses. And for that you need a particular process that allows you to see your business differently. If you are to uncover greater leverage, it's intuitive to look at operations from different angles and yet, time and time again I see little creativity and innovation brought to strategic thinking. It's not as widely practiced as it could be. One of the main reasons is that there is no methodology or discipline that fosters different thinking so ideas and innovation simply drift in the ether, never to be captured and converted. There are a number of reasons for this, but one of the main culprits is the folly of financial leverage. The age-old practice that seldom works: throw more money at the problem.

The goal

I've written this book and we have created a series of seminars on the *90% Rule* because so many companies have not moved beyond established thinking and learned how to leverage the low-risk, low-investment assets they already have. They have so much invested in "traditional assets," "customer capital" and "intellectual capital" and yet, they do not leverage this and exploit the opportunities within their reach. I believe there are a number of reasons:

This is not about "reorganizing," rather it is about relooking, rethinking, redoing. It's looking at strategic opportunities through a new set of lenses. And for that you need a particular process that allows you to see your business differently.

- They haven't thought about it (especially from an entrepreneurial perspective)
- They haven't made the time to do it
- They haven't had a clear understanding of how to do it
- They have no process for doing it.

My goal is to help you adopt and implement a customized process that can leverage all facets of your current capital investment and help you achieve a much higher level of sustained growth.

Hedgehogs and tortoises

I believe in the principle of hedgehogs and tortoises. Like the mythical story of the tortoise and the hare, I believe in winning the race, not chasing the next quick-fix. I believe in long-term sustainable growth, not short-term performance "hits." I believe in evolution, not revolution. Revolutions tend not to last long.

In the race for success, speed is less important than stamina. The sticker outlasts the sprinter.

Bertie Charles Forbes (1880-1954)
Founder, Forbes magazine

Remember, you're already 90% of the way to a better future and moving ahead has a great deal to do with how you view your business.

It is about uncovering opportunities that you are already 90% capable of achieving.

— Tencer and Cardoso

Chapter 3

Understand your core business
Then disturb the status quo

I'm not an entrepreneur. I like rules too much, and entrepreneurs break rules.

Guy Hands, CEO, Terra Firma Capital Partners

The reason you are in business in the first place is to disturb the status quo, "break the rules" and do something different. You want to seize an opportunity with both hands and shake the marketplace with it.

Most entrepreneurs start businesses because they see an opportunity to do something better, something different from the competition. By definition, the function of entrepreneurs is to disturb the status quo, to blaze a new trail.

But you can't begin to be different if you don't know who you are, what you do best (the 90%), what you could do to make a difference and know what's out there in the marketplace.

Most people don't take the time to figure out what business they are really in. For instance, can a gas station sell more than

But you can't begin to be different if you don't know who you are, what you do best (the 90%), what you could do to make a difference and know what's out there in the marketplace.

gas? Is the corner store in the business of selling milk, snacks, cigarettes or convenience and time? You can't differentiate on commodity products but you can on time and convenience. Two identical stores in different parts of town may be serving different customer needs and require different approaches (strategies) for growth. There are many different ways to leverage customer benefits like convenience and time. That's why we now see what used to be just a gas station turned into a convenience store with coffee and donuts, drive-thrus and ATM machines. It's even evident in the branding with the names like Mobil's "On the Run" service stations and for over forty years "7-Eleven."

If you don't understand your roots and what got you here and what your customers value, then it will be difficult to know which assets and ideas will get you to where you want to go.

> **"Would you tell me please, which way I ought to go from here?"**
> **"That depends a good deal on where you want to go."**
> **"I don't much care where."**
> **"Then it doesn't matter which way you go."**
>
> *Lewis Carroll,*
> *Author, Through the Looking Glass*

The good news is that there are countless examples of companies—big and small, famous and infamous—that have succeeded by figuring out what business they are really in. Have you?

True to your core

Disney has always been different—a step above and a step ahead of all the wannabe-Disney film studios and theme parks—and yet always true to its core business. Disney never lost sight of the power of leveraging what it was already good at. They know that they not only sell the dream, but the dream is rooted in the original entrepreneurial spirit of Walt Disney himself. He made sure the company's brain trust always remembered who they were and what they were good at and that they never veered far from simply improving and expanding on 90% of what they did best. "Walt's way" was anchored in four steps: "Dream, Believe, Dare, Do."[3]

We can learn from them all. From Apple and Disney to Harley-Davidson and Gap Adventures, growth is fueled by entrepreneurial thinking and the will to *cause a disturbance*® that is rooted in a core strength. It's not just the big guys; thousands of small and medium-size companies shake up their marketplaces every day.

> ### *When you see a successful business, someoneonce made a courageous decision.*
> *Peter Drucker*

Gap Adventures

Bruce Poon Tip started his own adventure-travel company, Toronto-based Gap Adventures, as a way of exploring his personal values. He had traveled through Thailand like a native, riding broken-down buses, staying in small, family-run hotels and eating local foods. Pitying the Western tourists with their air-conditioned motor coaches, he decided to launch his own company to help venturesome Westerners access authentic travel and cultural experiences through small-group trips to offbeat destinations around the world.

Today Gap Adventures is the world's largest adventure-travel firm with sales of more than $100 million, 100,000 customers

---

[3] *The Disney Way,* Capodagli and Jackson, p. xi

a year, and tours on all seven continents. Now respected as an international expert on eco-tourism, Poon Tip has never sacrificed his personal values for growth. But he has learned to think big and embrace multiple target markets.

Since his beginning selling tours to Thailand and the ruins of Machu Picchu in Peru, Poon Tip now sells more than 1,000 different tours. He realized early on that his company had to appeal to more than just backpackers even though his first brochure warned, "If you'd like all the comforts of home, we suggest you stay home."

Poon Tip's true target: anyone looking for an alternative to conventional tourism and three-star beach resorts. Today Gap targets high-income singles, families, photography buffs, gourmets, affluent retirees and other niche groups through a range of specialty tours – including a $13,000 voyage to Antarctica by icebreaker.

Gap grew by realizing that the product it's selling is not exactly travel but *experiences*. Satisfied customers sign up for Gap trips year after year because they trust the company to connect them to unique new adventures—in the company of like-minded travelers.

To reach this independent-minded market, Gap has pioneered new marketing techniques: abolishing "single supplements", conducting traveling slide shows to entice prospects and opening brick-and-mortar stores (in New York, Toronto, Vancouver and Melbourne) when the rest of the travel industry was focusing on the Internet. Gap produces its own television shows and online videos, and provides an online traveler's forum moderated by satisfied customers, not the company's staff. Gap has even created its own foundation, Planeterra, to build client relationships and "give back" to the communities Gap travelers visit.

With his company growing 30% a year, Poon Tip admits he is following no road map but instinct. "There's no precedent for a company of our size in this industry," he says. For his next act, he's considering expanding into book publishing, restaurants and hotels. But he has no interest in accepting the many offers he's received to sell his company. "I'm working hard, but I'm having more fun than ever."

Companies get away from their core business strengths for any number of reasons and two of the more common are that they lose sight of what their core business is; or in many cases, simply ignore it. Either way, it's never a happy ending. Most of the companies I have dealt with over the years fall into the first category and do not get back to their roots because they are stuck seeing themselves through the same old lens. They are mired in operational pressures and the pervasive thinking, "It's the way we've always done it."

> **If the only tool you have is a hammer, after a while everything begins to look like a nail.**
>
> Abraham Maslow (1908-1970),
> American psychologist

The first thing you have to do is take a different view of who you are and how you got to where you are today.

> **Know your core business, build on its strengths, break the rules and disturb the status quo.**
>
> — Tencer and Cardoso

Companies get away from their core business strengths for any number of reasons and two of the more common are that they lose sight of what their core business is; or in many cases, simply ignore it.

4

Your core business through a different lens

What you see depends on how you look at it.
Sometimes what we need is a different point of view.

How nickels can be worth more than dimes

Let me relate a story originally told by Edward de Bono, a renowned leader in creative thinking and the man who coined the term "lateral thinking." It goes directly to the point of seeing things differently in order to leverage unseen value. My bet is that the Tommy in this story will grow up to be an entrepreneur.

It's all in how you look at things

Tommy is five years old. Typically, he's in constant pursuit of his nine-year-old brother John. And John, like most older brothers, is always picking on Tommy. One day, John and two of his buddies are hanging out in his room when Tommy comes wandering in. John says to his buddies, "Hey guys, wanna get a laugh? Watch this." His friends eagerly gather around. "Tommy, come here."

Pleased with the invitation, Tommy breaks into a big grin and looks up with great anticipation. John sits down on the edge of the bed and holds out his hands, palms up. In his right hand is a dime and in his left a nickel. He glances back at his buddies and whispers, "Watch how stupid Tommy is." Turning, he flashes a know-it-all grin at his brother's innocent face. "Hey Tommy, which one of these coins do you want, the big one or the small one?" Tommy's eyes ponder his choices for just a moment. "This one." The little guy shoots out his hand, grabs the nickel, jams it in his pocket, and leaves the room.

John triumphantly closes his hand on the dime, breaks into a smug smile, and turns for approval from his buddies. The boys are in stitches. John stops chuckling long enough to say, "Is that stupid or what? He falls for it every time."

The laughter is cut short as a large shadow fills the doorway. It's John's father. "John, your brother is not stupid, and I don't want you playing that trick on him again. Do you hear me?" He gets a guilty reply. "Yeah, okay. We're just playing, Dad. Tommy doesn't care. He likes it." His father interjects sternly, "Well, I'll have no more of it and I'll speak to Tommy, too." He turns and heads for Tommy's room. "Hi, Tommy. How are you doing?" "Hi Dad." Tommy is sitting in the middle of his bedroom surrounded by Lego blocks.

"Tommy, I want to explain something to you." Lowering himself onto the floor, he leans back against the end of the bed. He then spends the next five minutes putting the value of nickels and dimes into context for his son. Using pennies, nickels, dimes and quarters, he shows his son that the size of the coin does not always represent the value of the coin. Throughout the chat, Tommy listens carefully and nods his head, "So, do you see the difference between a nickel and a dime?" asks his father. "Yeah. A nickel is 5 pennies and a dime is 10 pennies," he answers proudly. "Good," says his father. "So the next time John asks you to pick a coin, which one are you going to pick?" "The nickel," says Tommy.

Exasperation is all over the father's face. "No, Tommy, not the nickel, the dime. It's worth twice as much." Tommy reaches under his bed for an old sock and turns it upside down. Dozens of nickels fall out of the sock. "Yeah, but if I take the dime John will stop playing the game … and look how many nickels I've got from him!"

> ### *Tommy's audacity never fails to amaze me.*
> *Tommy's father*

Tommy understands leverage

New ideas form when we change the way we look at things (nickels can be worth more than dimes). The *90% Rule* is built on the premise of innovation: See differently. Think differently. Do differently. Even when it seems audacious.

The process: Six fundamental steps

What our little pictogram depicts is a whole new landscape. A place and process from which you can begin to see, think and act differently.

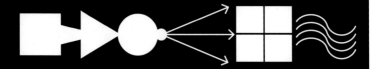

This little pictogram will change how you view your business.

The icons in the pictogram represent a six-step process that is a continuous loop that helps you see your business differently. It will trigger new ideas, open up new opportunities and increase your growth potential. It will identify, rank and map opportunities in markets, products and services that you are already 90% capable of providing.

This model is designed for businesses and not-for-profit organizations that want a systematic and manageable process for continuous growth. Implementation of the model requires two perspectives:

i) Your depth of inside knowledge, insight and thinking;

ii) An outside knowledge, objectivity, entrepreneurial thinking and systematic process.

Managed effectively, this process will turn the little pictogram into a whole new way of doing business.

Step One: ▪

Revisiting your company's origins and identify where you want to take it long-term.

Step Two: ▶

Exploring what you can be, not just what you are.

Step Three: ●

Building a relevant brand rooted in customer-centric thinking.

Step Four: ●⟨

Maximizing leverage by outlining your best opportunities and the criteria upon which to assess them.

Step Five: ▦

Building an opportunity matrix to determine the human and financial resources required for moving ahead.

Step Six: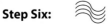

"Speaking" to be heard clearly by all your audiences.

A few of the outcomes

Sustained success accrues to companies that install the integrated process that applies the *90% Rule*. There are many benefits and outcomes for the companies that do this. A few examples:

- You clearly define what business you are in – from a customer viewpoint – including a clearly articulated and refined vision and mission for your company
- You establish the right context for strategic decision – making
- You redefine your core target markets and develop a clear position relative to your competition
- You define and assess a series of actionable and measurable opportunities
- You identify your communication goals and message to ensure that you are using the most relevant communication tools and always speaking clearly and consistently
- You build a systematic process that continually supports evolutionary long-term growth
- You consistently align action with strategy
- You continually uncover opportunities
- You get innovation on the front burner, every day, turning ideas into action on a regular basis
- You continually leverage limited resources

I know this seems like a lot to do (and a lot to promise), but the truth is, once you've institutionalized the process, innovative thinking will become as natural as getting out of bed. Identifying new opportunities, assessing them and getting them onto an action track will become second nature for your team. So as the song goes, "Take time to make time ..."

Rethink. Reinvent

When Indra Nooyi joined PepsiCo in 1994, she could see the venerable soft-drink and hospitality company was betting on the wrong horse. As the company's chief strategist, she helped steer a new course, helping PepsiCo sell off its artery-clogging fast-food brands (Taco Bell, Pizza Hut and KFC), and acquire more growth-oriented grocery assets, such as Tropicana juices and Quaker Oats (makers of Gatorade sports drinks, heart-healthy oatmeals and chewy granola bars).

Suddenly, PepsiCo was less about sugared drinks and snacks, and more about brand-name convenience foods – and nutrition. As PepsiCo's revenues and profits soared, Nooyi was promoted to president, then CEO and later company chairman. She is credited as chief architect of PepsiCo's multi-year growth strategy, Performance with Purpose, which focuses on creating innovative food products with "responsible nourishment," while minimizing impact on the environment. Specifically, Nooyi has pledged that half of PepsiCo's U.S. revenue will come from healthful products.

Putting its money where its mouth is, PepsiCo was one of the first big international food producers to eliminate trans-fats from its products. It has become a leader in campaigning against obesity and supporting agencies that promote access to safe drinking water worldwide.

Pepsico's transformation is good citizenship and good business. As Nooyi told CNBC in 2007, "Across the world we have unleashed the power of our people to come up with ideas to reduce, recycle, replenish the environment, and we are making great progress by reducing how much water we use in our manufacture and the carbon footprint that we put on the environment." Besides the financial benefit, she says PepsiCo has also become a more sought-after employer to the best new graduates, "They want to come to a company to work for a purpose."

PepsiCo's payoff? Sales have grown from $31 billion in 1996 to $43.3 billion in 2009. In 2005, its total market value exceeded arch-rival Coca-Cola's for the first time. In 2009, Nooyi was named CEO of the Year by the Global Supply Chain Leaders Group.

Recently, The Wall Street Journal asked Nooyi where she gets ideas for new products. Her answer: She stays close to her core consumers. "I do market tours all the time. Every weekend I hop in the car and go somewhere. I listen to kids talk about what they're consuming, what they're doing, what they're not doing. I read a range of things to keep in touch with cultural and lifestyle trends … the usual business press, but also People and Vanity Fair and anything close to the cutting edge of the culture."

"Brands never die," says Nooyi. "You only stop reinventing them."[4]

Rethinking, reinventing and innovation come from seeing your core business through a different lens, every day.

It may sound contradictory, but creative and innovative thinking needs discipline; a systematic process that can convert it into actionable opportunities.

— *Tencer and Cardoso*

---

[4] www.reveries.com/pepsichallenge, from *Wall Street Journal*, Sept. 11, 2008

Chapter

5

Getting innovative
thinking on the front burner

Innovation typically occurs at the interface of multiple disciplines.

Kenichi Ohmae, author
The Myth & Reality of the Japanese Corporation

Planning and time are in constant conflict in every business. Neither the business nor the world stops for planning and planning shouldn't stop every time the business or the world changes. It's a Catch-22.

As mentioned in the previous chapter, installing a process that can marshal the collective thinking of a business is central to success. Effective long-term planning comes from in-depth thinking, in-depth thinking comes from having enough time to think and having enough time to think comes from having a process that ensures it.

Problem: Time. Answer: Discipline

I know, the old discipline issue, but discipline is at the core of the time problem. Time is a continuum and every business tries to build processes to save precious time. But do they—do you—have a means for building *time to think* into every process, especially the process of business development?

It's not simply about making extra time. What is needed is a rigorous approach that ensures there is time for deeper thinking at every step along the way. When you create time to think, to consider problems and opportunities and options, you have a much better chance of converting corporate vision, goals and strategy into day-to-day innovation by everyone in the organization, from top to bottom. If you take the time to build and install the right process, your Return On Time (ROT) will be significant. And the change will be evident.

Thinking alone is not enough

It's not a shortage of ideas that holds organizations back; it's a lack of a pragmatic process for converting those ideas into action. We all spend a great deal of time thinking about opportunities but the issue is the right thinking at the right time and the right outcomes from that thinking.

Great thoughts often percolate while we're madly scrambling to complete the next project. They are often good ideas but they seldom get linked to vision, goals and strategy. And they seldom get implemented. Even when they do, it's usually too late because you're too far down the line and now you have to get on with selling something. Thinking alone achieves nothing until the best ideas are turned into opportunities, then innovative actions and then profitable sales and growth.

Balance—an elusive goal

The conflict between time and *time to think* always brings us to the eternal balancing act in business, balancing the short and long-term needs of the organization.

When you create time to think, to consider problems and opportunities and options, you have a much better chance of converting corporate vision, goals and strategy into day-to-day innovation by everyone in the organization, from top to bottom.

For me, in our business, whether it's working one-to-one to solve a client's immediate problem or making enough time to write this book, the process we use is geared to achieving a balance that meets the immediate demands of running the day-to-day business and the need to work on longer-term plans in a disciplined manner.

I begin by telling myself, "Balance or fall." Each morning when I wake up, I begin with three thoughts:

- What am I going to sell today?
- What's one thing I can do today to make my business better?
- How will the answers to these previous questions impact us in the long-term?

The challenge is consistently converting these thoughts into actions and results. And the gauntlet that I—and all of us—have to run every day threatens to undermine our good intentions.

Preparation is everything. Noah didn't start building the ark when it was raining.

Warren Buffett, American financier

In the beginning

Think about investor Warren Buffett and his celebrated focus on long-term results while he is making what must be a whole lot of short-term decisions. Consider the pressure he was under during the financial debacle of 2008-2009: When the market was cratering, Buffett bought $5 billion worth of Goldman Sachs stock (with another $5 billion in options)[5]. And then he bought a railroad—Burlington Northern Santa Fe for $26 billion.[6] Even for him these are decisions made in the heat of a short-term firestorm (sound familiar?). And since

[5] *Globe and Mail*, Sept. 14, 2009
[6] *Globe and Mail*, Dec. 1, 2009

he's got a pretty good track record, he's a relevant example of the importance of building balance into your business—even if you're dealing in millions instead of billions. The long term is an aggregation of a lot of short terms; therefore, what you do, or don't do, in the short-term eventually shapes your long-term.

What's on the front burner?

The hardest thing is to find the time to think innovatively about your own business. It's the old story about the shoemaker whose children had no shoes because he was so busy making shoes for others. We all live that story. Everything seems to be on the front burner—more shoes, more shoes, more shoes … except our children's shoes.

In many businesses, front burner issues eat up the vast majority of time and energy. Consequently, time is consumed in doing what has to be done, not thinking about what could be done. Two things always seem to be on the front burner:

- Things that pop up unexpectedly and jump to the front burner because they have to be dealt with immediately
- The ongoing daily pressures of meeting various performance metrics—everything from tracking and tweaking sales and profits to paring costs and meeting payroll

The only thing faster than the speed of change is the speed of thought.

D.H.Hughes, co-author Thoughtware

Moving innovation to the front burner

Experts have known, talked and written about innovation for decades and yet, most companies continue to struggle with how to generate more innovation. Not in the R&D department—many are good there (3M, Microsoft, Dell)—but in the day-to-day operations. Especially in small and medium size enterprises, where innovation is often an afterthought.

Part of the 21st century reality is that most companies no longer have the time to "think about," "sleep on," and "percolate" ideas before making a decision. The future is now. Technology has accelerated the rate of change to the point that it is nearly impossible to keep up. When it comes to the medium and long-term decisions, many companies simply can't make the best decisions because they have had no time to think about the future before it arrives. As a result, so many decisions have to be made out of context.

Today, your business is more complex, under more pressure, has shorter timelines and shrinking product life cycles. Today, damn near everything is on the front burner. The key to success is getting innovation there too.

Innovation: a fundamental principle

The infusion of innovative and entrepreneurial thinking into everyday business is a fundamental principle in our model. It allows you to build innovation and time to think into your normal routine. It's not about having an annual corporate retreat or a few one-off seminars because if you're waiting for months or a year to think about how to be more innovative, you are already being out-innovated by your competitors.

The easiest way to predict the future is to invent it.
Anonymous (Xerox Research Center)

If you have a thought about a new direction or opportunity your business should consider, then you need to find a way to explore it, acid-test it and create go/no go decisions that you can act on now—and measure later. The *90% Rule* allows you to continually deal with new opportunities and ideas as you do other front burner issues. It gives you a fighting chance to grow—continuously.

Thinking alone is not enough. You need a process that builds in time to think and innovate.

— *Tencer and Cardoso*

Chapter 6

Marketing and sales: Siamese twins

At some point somebody has to sell something.

I didn't want to leave this thought about *selling* something unaddressed because at the end of the day, the generation of profitable sales and a strong bottom line is everybody's goal. The thing is, success comes much easier when you sell the right stuff to the right people. That's why understanding your core business, your customers and your culture must drive the process of entrepreneurial thinking and innovation.

Too many people believe that sales are an investment and marketing an expense. Nothing could be further from the truth. That's why the road we take—this process—leads to better marketing to grow more sales more effectively. If you make a product, provide a service, charge one group of people to buy what you sell and look for ways to let more people know about your product, then you are already a marketer. But not until you have connected marketing and sales and invested equal amounts of thought and development in them

Too many people believe that sales are an investment and marketing an expense. Nothing could be further from the truth. That's why the road we take—this process—leads to better marketing to grow more sales more effectively.

do you open up the opportunity for your company to evolve as a great marketer and seller.

What's more expensive?

- Attempting to sell your products to disinterested or irrelevant prospects and throwing away buckets of money speaking to a blank wall (because marketing was never asked to figure out who to sell what to)?
- Or honing in on a smaller, more qualified group of prospects who are keenly interested in buying what you sell (because marketing figured out who they are, where they are, what they want and how to talk to them)?

Obviously, focus on the latter and build a lasting, mutually beneficial relationship with loyal customers.

We have all been on the receiving end of selling efforts devoid of any marketing intelligence. For a number of years, I received telemarketing calls from a company that assured me that they would get me top dollar if they sold my house. I lived in an apartment at the time. Oh, and there's that memorable call I received from a credit card company asking me why I had cancelled my gold card. Answer: Because they had issued me a platinum card. Obviously, nobody in the sales silo was talking to the marketing silo.

Siamese twins

Marketing 101 clearly sets out:

- The purpose of marketing is to develop a product or service; identify and qualify markets and customers; map the road to market; and define and create *effective* communications.
- The purpose of sales is to develop customer relations; deliver the force behind "closing sales"; provide

important market feedback; and directly impact the top-line (and middle-line) gross margins.

Everything I ever needed to know about selling ... was learning how to identify, find and keep customers.

Lillian Vernon, Catalogue retailer

The key is in the integrated thinking that connects sales and marketing. They are Siamese twins, not unrelated silos. First, it's important to ensure that the collective thinking throughout the company understands that investing in marketing is as important as investing in sales. Together they are a significant point of leverage; separately they offer little leverage.

One good funnel leads to another

Business colleague and "sales scientist," Adrian Davis, President and CEO, Whetstone Inc., for whom I have a high regard, has written extensively on the importance of sales and marketing working hand-in-hand. The following is a synopsis of some of his thinking.

Historically, there has been a divide between sales and marketing. Many companies have yet to get their sales and marketing teams working together seamlessly, whether business-to-business or consumer sales. However, the "new" economy is forcing the issue with more demanding buyers, more niche-oriented competitors and longer and longer sales cycles. Sales people are being forced to think more like marketers and marketing people are being forced to think more like sales people.

Both sales and marketing have their own funnels. Marketing must now directly tie the end of their funnel to the beginning of the sales funnel. Moreover, the output of the sales funnel

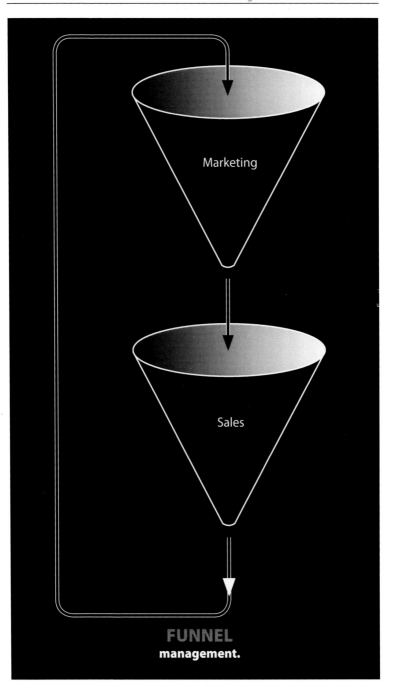

Marketing

Sales

FUNNEL
management.

must tie back into the marketing funnel. Every dollar spent on marketing must be measurable and show a return on investment. Every lead generated for the sales force must be accounted for.

Traditional marketing that only focuses on creating awareness in the marketplace doesn't work for most companies. The problem with this type of marketing is it can be expensive and not easily measured. Companies with big budgets tend to win this game. They succeed in creating mind share for the sales team to exploit, but they do so only by spending huge amounts of money. Moreover, they seldom know which specific initiatives led to their success. Today, CEOs and CFOs expect more from marketing. They are questioning every dollar spent. Good marketing executives get ahead of this scrutiny and know that marketing can be a great point of leverage.

Measure everything

They do so by carefully planning their programs and campaigns and setting up clear measurement criteria to determine which campaigns are successful and how to increase their effectiveness over time. These metrics include, but are not limited to: total reach, number of inquiries, number of first meetings, number of proposals, number of sales, meetings-to-reach ratio, closing ratio, conversion rate, acquisition cost, cost per contact, cost per click, cost per meeting, profit results and ROI. To measure these factors, marketers must clearly track all activity through the marketing funnel to the sales funnel. The marketing funnel should comprise three key stages:

1. **Reach:** The number of people in the potential base that will be touched by specifics program.
2. **Enquiry:** The number of people who respond positively by initiating contact.

3. **In consumer sales:** Who buys. In business–to–business: Getting a first meeting with qualified leads (i.e., people who are sufficiently interested that they are willing to meet with a salesperson to learn how the firm might address their specific challenges).

Every business-to-business campaign must be measured in terms of the number of first meetings it generates for the sales team. And every sales professional must be scrutinized in terms of his or her ability to convert first meetings into sales.

Linking funnels

The end of the marketing funnel is directly linked to the sales funnel. In business-to-business first meetings represent the top of the sales funnel. All activities prior to first meeting represent part of the marketing funnel, which sales people should be engaged in. (Yes, sales and marketing must learn to work together even more.) All opportunities must be tied to a specific campaign in order to connect sales and marketing activities. Once a first meeting is successfully concluded, the sales funnel should comprise three key stages:

1. **Diagnose:** The buyer is willing to work with the sales professional to help him or her understand the situation and develop a solution.

2. **Propose:** The consumer is clear on why they should buy. Or the B2B buyer is clear about the challenge they are facing, what your firm can do about it and is open to receiving clear documentation on the way you can work with them to fill their needs.

3. **Close:** The buyer, ready to take action to resolve his or her challenges, is now negotiating and completing necessary paper work to initiate a purchase.

Phases versus steps

The steps you go through to make a sale are not the same as the phases an opportunity will go through. Many organizations have more than a three-step sales process. Your sales process is not the same as your sales funnel phases. Managing the sales funnel is about managing the phases that opportunities go through as they mature. By way of analogy, what you do to harvest fruit is separate from the phases that fruit goes through as it matures. Fruit is initially unripe, then it ripens, and then it spoils if it's not eaten. The steps to harvest fruit might involve planting, tilling, spraying, inspecting, picking, etc. The steps you go through to harvest the fruit might be very different from mine, but the phases the fruit will go through are universal. The same principles apply to funnel management.

Wash, rinse, repeat

At the end of the sales funnel (surprise!) is the beginning of the marketing funnel. Existing customers must not be neglected. Aging customers are like aging accounts receivables. The older they get, the less likely you are to see any money come out of them. Marketing must now engage in a set of programs that reaches the entire client base, generates inquiries from existing clients and leads to new meetings with the sales team to discuss additional opportunities.

To make the most of your sales and marketing investment, accurate metrics must be gathered for each phase of the marketing and sales funnel. Getting a handle on these metrics and putting them into a management dashboard you can monitor at a glance is the key to ensuring that every dollar invested in sales and in marketing will provide increasing returns to the business. These metrics can be captured seamlessly if your CRM and accounting systems are set up properly and if your sales and marketing teams work together.

Once these metrics are tracked and managed, sales and marketing will have tied the knot—and you will have a cash-flow machine.

Sales and strategy: Two outcomes, one goal

Strategy for strategy's sake, to me, is a waste of time and money. "Strategy" is a term thrown around like a bad rumor. Everybody talks about it, but nobody knows quite what to do with it. The word "strategy" is worn out; it makes eyes glaze over. For insomnia it beats counting sheep. In my opinion, there is no greater killer of interest than starting off a seminar by saying, "Let's do a SWOT analysis (Strengths. Weaknesses. Opportunities. Threats)." Don't get me wrong, strategy is important; it's just misunderstood too often, especially in sales.

Although strategy drives critical outcomes, including sales, it too is an outcome. There are many different ways to arrive at strategies. I believe the most effective way is to install a process that is fully integrated into your business, not simply executed as a once-in-a-while undertaking (i.e., SWOT exercises) or as an isolated exercise for just sales or marketing. First, the process needs to engage the broadest scope of thinking in your company in terms of breadth of cross-functionality and in depth of thought. It must cover the full spectrum of your business, from origins to future opportunities. Secondly, the process should become an ongoing part of how you do business; continuously stimulating entrepreneurial thinking and creating innovation that drives sales.

Differences in B2B to consumer markets

One of the eternal divides in business is the difference between companies that sell to other businesses and those that sell to consumer markets. Often, the difference in scale, distribution and selling methods are as formidable as the obstacles that would prevent an Olympic sprinter from winning the gold in boxing. However, the transition can be made if there are common core competencies, and if you think of expanding innovatively: swimmer Michael Phelps might be able to become an Olympic diver, or sprinter Michael Johnson a 400-metre winner.

Breaking out

One company that has made that leap is OMI Industries of Chicago. It has taken the same deodorizing technology it developed for refineries, landfills and sewage plants and turned it into a "green" consumer product sold in high-end boutiques and specialty chains such as Ace Hardware and Whole Foods Market. Whether its customers are manufacturers, asphalt producers, pet owners or cigar smokers, "all buy the same technology," says OMI president Phil Coffey, "just in different forms."

Originally known as Odor Management Inc., OMI discovered a formula for using natural plant oils such as lime, anise seed, cedar and clove to attract and break down malodorous molecules. OMI's Ecosorb™ products actually eliminate bad smells, rather than mask them as most air fresheners do. OMI built a small but profitable business serving industrial clients until Coffey joined the company and suggested it explore consumer markets. He took years to convince the then-owners: they saw OMI as an industrial products company, while Coffey realized it was an innovator whose brands could reach every household in America.

He knew the job would be tough. Ecosorb would have to be reformulated into scores of different products. And instead of meeting clients one-on-one through plant visits or trade shows, the company would have to create new relationships with wholesalers and retailers.

In 2003, Coffey prepared his staff for the makeover by warning they could expect no raises for the next three years—and offering shares in the company as an incentive. Ever since, he has poured all of OMI's profits into producing new "Fresh Wave™" products (gels, candles, sprays, laundry additives and pet shampoos), with eye-catching packaging. By 2005, the brand was in 3,000 stores; by 2009 it was in 10,000.

Better still, becoming marketing-focused helped OMI develop new products for its industrial markets, as well as selling to major commercial businesses: in mid-2009 Hertz Car rental began using Fresh Wave products to neutralize rental-car odors at 1200 locations. "The technology OMI is providing us will enable us to keep our cars on the road longer," said a Hertz spokesman. "We'll have less downtime due to cleaning issues" – and fewer customer complaints about lingering food and tobacco smells.

By 2008, Fresh Wave revenues had reached $5 million—finally equaling the sales of OMI's industrial division. After years of effort, Coffey's consumer revolution is finally in the driver's seat.

Despite differences, sales and marketing are co-dependent so the task is to make them part of the same process and have them work seamlessly together.

Sustained growth is dependent on marrying and leveraging the innovative capabilities inherent in marketing and sales.

— *Tencer and Cardoso*

Chapter 7

Getting thinking to work

No one can possibly achieve any real and lasting success or "get rich" in business by being a conformist

J. Paul Getty (1892-1976), American industrialist

I said at the outset that this book is not about being an entrepreneur; it's about entrepreneurial thinking, which helps develop a collective mindset that can significantly leverage your current assets. It's about doing and making it work.

I remember the meeting well. I was sitting with an entrepreneur and potential client. She was a bright, articulate woman and she had created a good product that was just beginning to build traction in the marketplace. She was talking to a number of people to see what might be the "easiest" way to take the company to the next level. There were a number of options open to her. The first was to raise capital and open her own plant, but she did not want the financial risk. The second was to find a plant overseas and have them manufacture the product for her. She pointed out that this would entail a lot of due diligence, travel and personal time spent overseeing quality control in another country. She did not want to spend much time abroad. So her question to me was, "What do you think I should do?"

I thought about it for a New York minute. As hard as I searched my instincts and experience, I could only come up with one answer: "Go to bed, get a good night's sleep and when you wake up, go find a job."

It's attitude

On the surface, this may seem glib or rude. But it really isn't. It's about the entrepreneurial attitude, mindset and will that drives us to make a difference. The truth is—any entrepreneur knows it well—that running a business (yours or someone else's) means sacrifice, risk and uncertainty. If you find the inconvenience of travel or fear of risk a constant consideration, then I ask, "What are you doing in business?" Because where I come from, success comes from the heart, the attitude and the will you bring to every problem, every day. If it isn't there, you might as well stay in bed.

> ### *One person with a belief is worth ninety-nine with just an interest.*
> *John Stuart Mills (1806-1873) British philosopher*

Montreal entrepreneur Charles Sirois, the chairman of the Canadian Imperial Bank of Commerce (2009), is an atypical banker. He has started more than 20 businesses. He calls entrepreneurship "an attitude where you are ready to live with a certain amount of risk … so that you can face adversity and grow."[7]

The key is to know yourself. And know your tolerance level for risk, uncertainty and sacrifice because they're all part of the entrepreneurial equation. Your capacity to balance them and transform them into success is the reason you get out of bed every morning. And you chart your long-term path and choose your every day actions accordingly. You don't have to be running your own business. Many corporate executives make decisions and take risks that have real consequences to their organizations' growth and the same entrepreneurial thinking is required.

Having built a manufacturing firm, I know the risk inherent in securing capital to finance everything from operations, inventory and equipment. This isn't for everyone. But it has given me the hands-on understanding needed to find the maximum leverage in what I already have in order to grow a business.

It's audacity

As mentioned earlier, I believe audacity is the entrepreneurial thinker's best friend and at its core is a powerful part of self-reliance and independence. Many, if not most, of the history-changing entrepreneurs have had a large dose of audacity: Johannes Gutenberg, Alexander Graham Bell, Thomas Edison, Henry Ford, Bill Gates (a Harvard dropout), Steve Jobs, Jeff Bezos (for years the experts said Amazon.com was not viable), Sir Richard Branson and T. Boone Pickens (from oil to wind energy), to name a few. And, of course, tremendous change has always been delivered by the tens of thousands of lesser-known names, all of whom have had the audacity to go where others would not.

The only way to discover the limits of the possible is to go beyond them into the impossible.

Sir Arthur C. Clarke (1917-2008)
British author, inventor, futurist

For you and most people in your organization, there are a few entrepreneurial characteristics to look for:

- If you don't believe in yourself and your ideas then you can be sure nobody else will
- If you don't have passion for your business, it won't come from anybody else
- If it was supposed to be easy, everybody would be doing it
- The problems you face are not there to stop you from succeeding, but to stop others from going where you go
- If there are but a few words to live by, let them be vision, belief, audacity, persistence and will

No secret handshakes

I can't begin to tell you how often I've heard people ask what might be the key to being a successful entrepreneurial thinker. It's as if they believe there is a secret handshake taught as a part of business hazing and they can learn it and become a part of the entrepreneurs' club. Well, I don't know of any such secret or club. And from my discussions and work with countless entrepreneurs, from many different countries, if any of them knew of a secret formula or an off-the-shelf recipe, they weren't kind enough to share it with me. As I have discovered, it's much more than some manufactured methodology.

I had an interesting experience at a recent marketing roundtable that I was leading for a fast-growing manufacturer of branded and private label products. The founder and CEO was in the session, along with members of the management and sales teams. One of the "sticky" points brought up by management was that the entrepreneur did not share enough of his ideas in advance. He consistently held his cards close to his chest. This made it difficult for managers to make the day-to-day, tactical decisions that would contribute to the firm's long-term strategic direction. In response, the owner's candid and somewhat surprising opinion resonated with me. And it still does to this day.

He said, "I don't always share my ideas with everyone because in the past, when I have, there has been too much negative reaction and people saying why the idea couldn't or wouldn't succeed." He found the responses to be a deterrent, demotivating rather than motivating and usually dead wrong. This from a man who had successfully built and sold one business and was building another that was on a fast track to surpass $100 million in annual revenues.

I think the majority of us who understand the underpinnings of entrepreneurial thinking can share his sentiment. I know that I do. And I can't think of one successful entrepreneur I have met who doesn't know that negative "can't-do" thinking kills ideas, even coming from the bottom up. Entrepreneurs can't succeed without an unwavering commitment to their own ideas and beliefs. To them, the question isn't "if," but "how". This particular CEO and entrepreneur was curtailing the potential of his company because he could not get his people to leverage his innovative thinking. His goal was to change the culture and we helped them install the process and not longer after significant new thinking began to emerge.

Whether you think you can, or you can't, you will probably be right.

Henry Ford II (1917-1987)
Chairman & CEO, Ford Motor Company

I've heard a lot of "yeahbuts" in the course of business, and none expressed with greater certainty than when a client or prospective client says, "Yeahbut, our business is different." Of course, there are differences, but in the fundamental principles and processes that I'm talking about, there is little to no difference in their applicability to businesses of all sizes, shapes, colors and functions.

Beyond my first-hand knowledge, there are endless examples of the entrepreneurial spirit. I'm sure a couple of guys building the first, user-friendly personal computer in their garage must have had a few naysayers. In 1983, when Apple's Steve Jobs issued his edict to create the best possible PC software, he had little support for his vision. Even pioneers such as Bill Gates didn't see the extent of the opportunities. In the early eighties Gates said, "I think 640k ought to be enough for anyone." And Ken Olsen, chairman of Digital Equipment Corporation, in 1977 infamously quipped, "There is no reason for any individual to have a computer in his home." And Fred Smith's FedEx next-day courier concept, developed when he was in university, was summarily panned.

Yeahbut

I've heard a lot of "yeahbuts" in the course of business, and none expressed with greater certainty than when a client or prospective client says, "Yeahbut, our business is different." Of course, there are differences, but in the fundamental principles and processes that I'm talking about, there is little to no difference in their applicability to businesses of all sizes, shapes, colors and functions. Leverage is leverage, marketing is marketing, selling is selling, innovation is innovation, and they all come together when you create a common context for strategic decision-making. The key is discovering, defining and building within that context. That is where the 90% meets the 10%. That's where the old view and the yeahbuts transform into a new view and new growth.

Diamonds are created under pressure

My own businesses are typical examples. I have never had the opportunity to start or build a company with an excess of cash. My partners and I have always done it the old-fashioned way—with a bucket, a paddle and a couple of credit cards. In the beginning years, it's like a recession every day. But it's a great way to start because it encourages three behaviors that are requisite to success:

    i) A fundamental understanding of your business;

    ii) Ingenuity—entrepreneurialism;

    iii) Leverage—exploiting every advantage you can find.

All of these tactics can be more productive and valuable than cash. I use the metaphor that diamonds are made under pressure.

This is actually where we first refined the *90% Rule*—the need to grow a business from an existing base of expertise, equipment and limited capital. But we didn't think of "capital" as simply cash. We knew there was great value in other assets, especially the non-traditional ones (e.g., people, ideas, time). Because of this we have always asked and continue to ask ourselves: What new product or service can we leverage based on what we already have, what we already do, or what we already *almost* do?

In our current business, this helped us change from thinking of ourselves as just a strategy and design firm to one focused on cultivating entrepreneurial thinking in organizations of all sizes. We stopped defining ourselves in terms of the products and services we offered and focused on the customer-centered benefit—*helping companies pursue greater growth by understanding and leveraging the power of entrepreneurial thinking.* As part of this transformation, we have restructured the company into multiple operating platforms (business units) that meet the more specialized needs of our clients and each still remains closely integrated in cross-platform thinking, planning and execution.

In the beginning years, it's like a recession every day. But it's a great way to start because it encourages three behaviors that are requisite to success: i) A fundamental understanding of your business; ii) Ingenuity—entrepreneurialism; iii) Leverage—exploiting every advantage you can find.

For example, one of the strategic shifts we have made is from providing only one-to-one services to also offering one-to-many services (i.e., seminars, on-line networks and books). All are based on the same existing pool of knowledge (intellectual capital), but we have repackaged it to share with a greater community of thinkers. This enabled our business to grow with manageable capital requirements.

Innovation is applied creativity.

We understand that creativity is only the first half of innovation. Innovation happens when creativity is applied and converted into an actionable and measurable opportunity. The key lies in how to convert it.

It is through this process and the redesign of our business model that we have been able to continually reinvent ourselves and provide clients with the capability to reinvent their organizations.

Rethink to reunderstand to reinvent

We are all creatures of habit and the way we think might be the most ingrained habit known to humankind. The famous saying of 16th century philosopher René Descartes, "I think; therefore I am," might be more relevant in our scenario, if it said, "I think; therefore I must do." If we are to change behavior (the doing), we must change understanding, if we are to change understanding, we must change the thinking, and if we are to change the thinking, we must take a disciplined approach that helps us see "what is," perceive "what could be," and discover "how to achieve it."

Obviously, we all spend a lot of time thinking and doing but what I'm talking about is about doing things differently. It's not easy. But we make no apologies (our clients have never asked for one) for having the audacity to push people to change the way they think.

There is nothing man won't do to avoid the difficult task of thinking.

Thomas Edison (1847-1931),
American scientist, inventor, businessman

Unfortunately, no matter how much or how creatively you think, there is no way to know if what you are planning to do is going to work. That's the entrepreneurial risk every business has to live with. We're not talking about "winging it," we're talking about bringing together thinking and action in a methodology that mitigates risk by moving along a path that is systematically in tune with your vision, goals, strategy and customer needs.

It's a process, albeit a demanding one, that systematically corrals "blue sky" thinking, moves it toward stated goals and molds it into actionable, measurable opportunities that drive sales and growth.

There is no shortage of creative people in business. The shortage is of innovators. All too often people believe that creativity alone leads to innovation. It doesn't.

Theodore Levitt (1925-2006)
American economist, professor Harvard Business School

Trust the process

In this age of expectations over effort, quick-fixes over deliberation and activity over thought, it's a waste of time looking for the best secret handshake or the next so-called revolutionary business panacea. But if you're looking for sustainable change and evolutionary growth, then the *90% Rule*

In this age of expectations over effort, quick-fixes over deliberation and activity over thought, it's a waste of time looking for the best secret handshake or the next so-called revolutionary business panacea. But if you're looking for sustainable change and evolutionary growth, then the *90% Rule* gives you a pragmatic, proven process that marshals thinking and action into sustained growth.

gives you a pragmatic, proven process that marshals thinking and action into sustained growth.

Bring audacity, a notepad and ideas, and let's get to work exploring how you can finesse your organization into a true innovation-driven business that will change the lives of your customers.

Build a disciplined, collaborative, innovative process and infuse it with entrepreneurial thinking and you will create a driving force for sustainable growth.

— *Tencer and Cardoso*

Part
Two

**Working through
the *90% Rule*™**

Introduction

The best place from which to understand that the world is round is the moon. Understanding your business from a visionary level will help you clearly see the next, logical opportunities for growth.

I have always liked the saying, "The best place from which to understand that the world is round is from the moon" because the same counterintuitive insight is found in the *90% Rule*: To best understand the pragmatic steps required to achieve your greater vision, you need your first step to be from a higher, broader view. If you really want to explore and uncover the best opportunities, it is important to first look across the entire spectrum, considering not just what you see today but what you might imagine the future to hold. Through this process, you can move from the big picture to well-defined, specific opportunities that are actionable and measurable. The big picture encompasses vision, mission, goals and positioning and the process deals with them in a natural evolutionary way.

Much of what we do is about opportunity—uncovering it, seizing it, converting it.

From Webster's dictionary:

Opportun' ity noun: a favorable juncture of circumstances, a favorable occasion, a good chance.

From Spyder Works' lexicon:

Opportun' ity noun: whatever you believe, can be.

Each of these definitions of opportunity is suitably ambiguous, and so they should be. An opportunity is what you define it to be and this will differ by the needs of your customers and the type of product or service your company offers. Or the type of societal change that your not-for-profit organization is committed to bringing about.

Opportunities exist on many levels and while we can't define your opportunities for you, we can help you understand the levels that you must be able to think through in order to arrive at the opportunities that best suit your organization. At the beginning, there are top-level opportunities that encompass vision and mission. Then we move to the second, more defined level, identifying the most lucrative target groups with whom you must establish key positioning relative to your competition. Finally, we distill further and convert specific opportunities into projects that are actionable and measurable. This moves you from blue sky, vision and strategy (moon view) to down-to-earth pragmatic action.

It is an integrated process that involves continually exploring and developing new opportunities through a cycle of innovating, leveraging and implementing.

Chapter

8

■

Step One
Revisiting your roots to
create new growth

Foresight grows from insight

Foresight is everything. That's why we begin with hindsight

There are numerous studies and books that, in my loose interpretation, tell us that individual decisions are based, consciously or subconsciously, on the collectivity of our life's experience. So based on this principle, we start our process by exploring the past.

Looking back helps you identify the driving forces behind growth and you are able to identify the key motivating factors that led to the start of the business, the launching of products, and the adding of incremental services. This important first step rips away the veneer of today's day-to-day mindset and allows you to see the rational and emotional building blocks of the business and the entrepreneurial passion and insight that fueled it. Inspiration always has a starting point and where you will be tomorrow can draw heavily on the origins of that spark.

Every business success—whether rooted in how the company got started or in some of its later successes—begins as an idea in someone's mind and transforms into the vision and courage needed to make it happen. It requires a mix of intuition, insight, foresight, headache-splitting thinking and the sheer will to execute it.

If you want to succeed you should strike out on new paths rather than travel the worn paths of accepted success.

Anita Roddick, founder, The Body Shop

Every business success—whether rooted in how the company got started or in some of its later successes—begins as an idea in someone's mind and transforms into the vision and courage needed to make it happen. It requires a mix of intuition, insight, foresight, headache-splitting thinking and the sheer will to execute it. Those who do this successfully are, alas, exceptions to the rule, but what is *not* the exception is the process and where it begins. When you revisit how you got to where you are today, you will nearly always find the "gems," the ideas and insights that made the difference.

The story of one of our clients, Rock Wood Casual Furniture, illustrates my point of uncovering the inspiration.

Jennifer Mulholland is founder and President of RW Industries Ltd., operating as Rock Wood Casual Furniture. RW was founded in 1992 and has since become a regular on the *W100* list published by *Profit* magazine, "the definitive list of Canada's Top Women Entrepreneurs."

In 1991, Jennifer was between jobs and decided to travel to the Far East to visit a long-time friend. During that trip, Jennifer was struck by the richness and expression of the traditional local cultures. In particular, she was taken by the richness of their creations, the textures and the melding of materials—woods and metals—that were explored and crafted into their furnishing.

To help pass the time on the long flight back, Jennifer was reading a variety of house and home magazines and as she perused the "offerings" she realized that furniture sold for the backyard was simply boring in its design. And the range of products was inherently limited. Everything seemed aimed either at the low-end, created from cheap, disposable materials, or at the very high-end: utilitarian products offering "lifetime" guarantee. There seemed to be no middle ground and certainly nothing to tap the imagination of the consumer.

Having a strong background in marketing and design, Jennifer knew, then and there, what she would do next in her career: Create a design-inspired line of outdoor furniture based on rich, exotic woods that enhanced and transformed the backyard into a true extension and expression of the home— all at an accessible price-point.

Says Jennifer Mulholland, "I have found that inspiration comes at different times and in many ways. Unfortunately, we are not always open to it when it does appear – and the opportunity is lost. I now tend to leap and think later. It can be dangerous – but never dull."

As we go through our model, you will note that the key in Jennifer's history was strongly the emotional stage. It hinged on the intuitive recognition of connecting specific benefits to the customer's emotional needs for beauty, comfort and value. Understanding the emotional component is critical because too often, too many of us think only from a linear or chronological perspective and miss the emotional links. From Jennifer's overview she saw the emotional void in the outdoor furniture market.

History in three parts

The first goal is to develop a collective understanding of your company's history and evolution and as part of this process we look at your history from three points of view: chronology, emotion and revenue. This then forms the basis for "blue sky thinking.

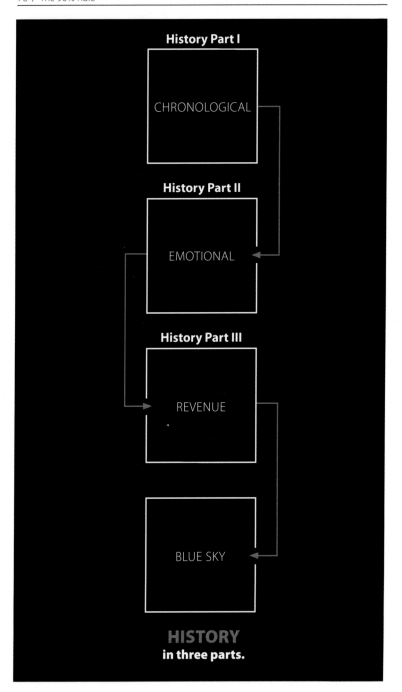

History Part I

CHRONOLOGICAL

History Part II

EMOTIONAL

History Part III

REVENUE

BLUE SKY

HISTORY
in three parts.

Part I: Chronological history

Your chronological history provides a foundational timeline that allows everyone to see clearly the growth and development of the firm. It gives you a record of key dates; changes and introductions of products and services; important points of reference; and major shifts in the company's history. From this you can create a collective perception of how the company became what it is today. Inherent in this is an examination of its strengths and weaknesses and the opportunity to explore ways of generating growth in the future.

Part II: Emotional history

Emotions are an underlying driver of a company and its culture. It's essential that everyone understand the genesis of the company's inspiration and emotional drive. From this, everyone can become more emotionally engaged in the company's goals and vision, which in turn, fuels the individual entrepreneurial spirit.

This process also allows you to find out how employees perceive the company, why they joined and why they are here. To maximize leverage, it is not enough to just have the viewpoint of the founder or CEO, or even a handful of leaders; it must come from everyone. Employees, especially those who have been there for many years, are an invaluable part of the firm's "memory" and can provide emotional insights on the history and growth. This is key in mapping a new way forward.

Part III: Revenue history

Revenue history reveals future potential and pitfalls. Understanding the source of revenues and profits across your history allows you to look forward and assess whether these sources are likely to grow or be gone in the future. You can see trends, patterns and anomalies that tell the story about what you did and didn't do, and how the company got to where it is today. You also explore factors behind the trends like technology, law, product life cycle, changing markets, innovation.

A historic revenue picture provides a platform on which everyone can combine past and future thinking as you explore possibilities and opportunities. Too often we either get stuck in present thinking or leap too quickly to future thinking when what is needed first is thinking that is grounded in a thorough understanding of history.

The reason your vision of the future starts with a visit to your past is because you need it in order to understand the 90% you are already capable of doing. From this perspective, everyone can begin to envision a different future and see the potential for building stepping-stones to get there. This gives you the necessary foundation for "blue skying" that is relevant versus haphazard (useless).

Background for blue skying

The historical record is the common denominator on which everyone can "blue sky" the future, which we do in step two (Chapter Nine). However, while you are reviewing your history it is valuable to discuss and make notes on future "considerations" even before you get deep into exploring and blue skying. As you go, pose such questions as:

- Where do you see the future of the business?
- What new things might customers need?
- What new customers might we need?
- How do you see us getting there?
- What would we need to resource that?

The purpose is to open up minds to entrepreneurial thinking.

Vision is the art of seeing what is invisible to others.

Jonathan Swift (1667-1745)
Irish satirist, essayist, author, Gulliver's Travels

Hypothetical objectives

Most companies have established specific objectives—financial, marketing, sales—which at this stage we call "hypothetical objectives." The reason is simple. This process puts all your objectives, strategies and tactics through a rigorous series of "tests" that are based on customer-centric benefits, market-centric strategies and existing assets; therefore, until they are "tested" they are considered hypothetical.

The hypothetical objectives give you a baseline to work from. They can be as ambitious as you like, but it is important to also make them pragmatic. Don't talk about expanding into twenty new countries in the next three years or doubling the business every six months unless you believe that there is a good chance to achieve it. In turn, don't set easy objectives that can lead to complacency. Both are ultimately demotivating.

As you proceed, the approach in your blue sky thinking will be set out in three timeframes: 1 year; 3 – 5 years; 10 years. The objectives can stem from many facets of the business and will include such things as:

- Corporate revenue
- Revenue by division or product
- Revenue growth rate
- Market share
- New market penetration
- Customer base
- Geographic growth

With history in hand and a range of hypothetical new objectives, it's time to broaden the exploration.

Remember, you can see the future better if you first take a step back and look at your history.

— *Tencer and Cardoso*

Chapter 9

Step Two
Exploring what you can be, not what you are

You've got to think about the big things while you're doing the small things, so that all the small things go in the right direction.

Alvin Toffler,
American writer and futurist

The crucible for entrepreneurial thinking is the exploratory mind and its incessant questioning: "What if?" "Why not?" As the view turns from the past to looking at the potential, entrepreneurs constantly ask, "What can be?"

Entrepreneurs and innovators are ahead of the curve, ahead of the market, ahead of current thinking; whereas, good managers are just slightly ahead of current thinking; average managers demonstrate current thinking; and managers who are behind the curve, lose.

For example, the traditional approach to rebranding is based on trying to understand "what the company is," and then coming up with a corporate identity and pithy slogan to

Entrepreneurs and innovators are ahead of the curve, ahead of the market, ahead of current thinking; whereas, good managers are just slightly ahead of current thinking; average managers demonstrate current thinking; and managers who are behind the curve, lose.

communicate that current state. Our methodology generates far more insight, and is more pragmatic. It explores *what you can be* versus simply *what you are*.

For instance, taking your company from sales of $50 million to $100 million in five years usually requires more than adding a blue chair to your product line and a new slogan to your brochure. At this point in the process, we want to understand benefits, particularly the benefits your company is already 90% capable of delivering to its customers. And how those benefits can solve customers' problems and change their lives.

I have discovered, over and over, that success is rooted in what you believe your business can be and do, not in the features and benefits of your current products or services. This exploration stage is about pursuing those beliefs and transforming the passion that got you here into renewed bigger benefits for your customers.

Benefit-driven thinking

The outcome from this collective exploration is a "cluster of benefits" that are anchored in what your customers want and need. This is the platform on which corporate vision, strategic intent and blue sky ideas fuse together to open up new opportunities. Customer-centric thinking (versus product/service-centric) means it is not about what you do or make, but what the customer wants and does (in their life or business). Most companies have an inherent product-centric bias that can be difficult to shed. That is why exploring and understanding the customer-centric perspective opens up a broader and clearer view of *what could be*.

What business are you really in?

Big question. Many companies have difficulty answering it correctly. The exploring and prioritizing of benefits allows you

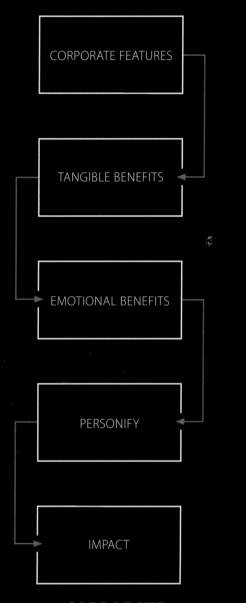

CORPORATE FEATURES

TANGIBLE BENEFITS

EMOTIONAL BENEFITS

PERSONIFY

IMPACT

CORPORATE
features and benefits model.

to clearly define or redefine the business you are in. Then you can blue sky where you might be able to go and match *what you can be* with *where you want to go*. The blue sky is like the wide end of a funnel, the beginning of the process where all possibilities are considered. From this comes the creation of vision and mission statements.

You are in the business of providing benefits. Some of these benefits are obvious, while others are less apparent and yet, just as important. Still others have been lost in the push and pull of growth and the day-to-day operational scramble. Applying the *Corporate Features and Benefits Model*, you can look at the benefits you think your products and services provide to your customers.

In this model, a company's features are the full offering of the products and services that it offers to its customer, not the specific features of each product or service. The continuum that we are building is on the left.

Now, let's explore the corporate features and benefits.

1) What are the main *products and services (corporate features)* that you are selling to your customers? (Seminars, books, cars, hedge trimming. List them all)

2) What are the key *tangible benefits* of your company, products and services? Define them clearly and as specifically as possible (drive faster, last longer, taste better, higher resale value, pay in 15 months, etc.).

3) What are the key *emotional benefits* that customers derive from your company, products and services? Essentially, what ego satisfaction do they achieve by using your product or service? Define them clearly (trend setters, belong to an "in group," perceive to be more intelligent, better educated, in-the-know, feel good about how they look, etc.).

4) Once you've explored all the features and benefits of your products from a customer perspective, then you *personify* them. Ask the team participating in the exercise how they would personify the business or brand in terms of key characteristics. This is done by naming well-known things or people that participants feel have similar characteristics to the brand/company (strength, elegance, function, cost, etc.). For example: Cars (Mercedes or Chevrolet); Animals (Lion or Cheetah); People (celebrities); Movies; Songs; etc.

5) Review your findings from these exploratory steps and then distill them into a brand *impact statement* that summarizes your brand's full customer benefits (e.g., help people to live better longer, become a social, moral and ethical compass for business, help parents to live guilt-free, providing the feeling of living the good life).

Examples of how benefits become impact statements:

- Revlon is not about making cosmetics; it's about selling hope
- Wellpoint is not about providing medical services; it's about helping people to live better longer
- *Today's Parent* magazine is not about family reading; it's about helping parents to live with less guilt
- Disney is not about movies and theme parks; it's about family entertainment.
- Starbucks is not about coffee; it's about a socializing lifestyle.

Vision. Mission. Impact

Now, with your customer-centric thinking and benefits in hand, you can build a bridge from what you are already offering to what you believe *you can be* by defining your vision, mission and brand statement. From the benefits you develop a summary *Impact Statement* as to how the benefits change customers' lives and this statement allows you to take a step back and refine or rewrite the vision and mission statements for your business. Once you understand the impact that your company makes in the marketplace, your vision and mission will become that much easier to articulate.

Defining vision and mission

It is critical to understand the difference between a vision and mission statement. All too often, I find they are not properly understood and written. Remember, these are statements (not autobiographies). You want them to be clear, concise and memorable.

Below are excerpts from what I found to be one of the clearest explanations, which came from Bill Birnbaum, CMC, as he presented to the American Management Association and published on-line at www.birnbaumassociates.com.

> **Vision Statement:** "… a vision is not true in the present, but only in the future. Your strategy team will need to develop a compelling vision of the future. A vision that your employees will enthusiastically embrace—because the vision is worthy and because it challenges them to grow."

> **Mission Statement:** "… your mission describes what business you're in and who your customer is. As such, it captures the very essence of your enterprise— its relationship with its customer … mission has both an internal and an external dimension … it also lists the functions the company performs … also includes the necessary external dimension. It identifies the

customer ... and it cites the company's "market position"—the reason why customers would prefer to buy products and services from the company."

Sticking to—versus getting back to—your core business

Once you have defined your brand impact, vision and mission, you are beginning to clearly understand and better define your core business. It's an essential cornerstone on which to build growth and a better place to be than always working at "getting back to our core business," which usually follows the folly of fragmented strategies and ill-planned diversification or malignant mergers. A much better approach to a growth strategy is to continually revisit, explore, reinvent and renew your core business.

Now that you have defined your high-level opportunities, you are going to be refining and moving closer to a list of actionable, measurable opportunities that are in keeping with your vision and focused on your best opportunities.

A few who understand

Disney

Where would Disney be if Walt had thought that the company's product was a comic book rather than seeing the company as being in the business of family entertainment (short for movies, TV, theme parks and retail stores). What has been called "the Disney Way" came from adherence to four basic principles as set by Walt himself: *Dream, Believe, Dare, Do* (this goes back to understanding the roots of your inspiration). Walt lived this credo and yet, he realized there was no real "pixie dust" for making things happen. He knew it was about stepping up to the plate and being willing to swing the bat.[8] And doing it consistently, at every level of the business, by building a brand based on consumer-centric benefits. Disney still lives by that magic of entrepreneurial passion and vision—along with a rigorous adherence to delivering more and more customer benefits by creating innovation around 90% of their core capabilities. Even the town, Celebration, that they built is conceived from the original vision, mission and brand.

Apple

Where would Apple be if Steve Jobs and Steve Wozniak had not first thought about redefining the concept of the personal computer? What if they had accepted the assumption of the times that computers were massive, expensive machines unsuited for individual use? And where would Apple be today if it had just thought of itself as a manufacturer of personal computers rather than creating design-enhanced personal technology (iPod and iPhone). They didn't just redefine their business, they redefined an industry.

lululemon

lululemon is a culture of well-being; not an article of clothing. Its mission states the company's primary intent: *Creating components for people to live a longer, healthier, more fun life.* Notice, no mention of athletic clothing itself. And take a look at their core values listed below—they see themselves as much more than a manufacturer and vendor of clothing.

lululemon core values[9]

Quality: Our customers want to buy our product again.

Product: We create components designed by athletes for athletes.

---

[8] *The Disney Way*, Capodagli and Jackson, p. xii

[9] lululemon website, www.lululemon.com

Integrity: We do what we say we will do when we say we will do it. If we cannot keep our promise, we immediately contact all parties and set new by-when dates.

Balance: There is no separation between health, family and work. You love every minute of your life.

Entrepreneurship: We treat and pay employees as though they run their own business.

Greatness: We create the possibility of greatness in people because it makes us great. Mediocrity undermines greatness.

Fun: When I die, I want to die like my grandmother who died peacefully in her sleep. Not screaming like all the passengers in her car.

Home Hardware

Home Hardware, a Canada-wide retailer, exemplifies the success that accrues from having recognized a growing market and building on what you already do by adding an innovative twist that better serves your market. Years ago they recognized the growth in the do-it-yourself (DIY) market and tapped into this trend by offering to help people help themselves by providing information and guidance. They became a leader in the Canadian home DIY market—instead of continuing to be just another supplier of commodity hardware products, competing on price and location.

Nutrition House

Nutrition House has pioneered the natural health and wellness industry and for the past 23 years the company has built its credentials through scientific research, quality ingredients and expert in-store counseling. Nutrition House provides the health information, products and services you need to make sound nutritional decisions about your life. To be a pioneer like Nutrition House, you must position your company beyond just selling products. It's not about the products, it's about where customers live, every day. The company positions itself as understanding and "proposing" a different way of living and eating. This alternative approach involves living life in a proactive way and applying natural solutions rather than the traditional "hope-you-feel-better" panacea of modern medicine. Strategically, this has helped Nutrition House leverage its knowledge and expertise into larger-format stores, international distribution of its products and extended product offerings including healthier food choices and ready-to-enjoy natural snacks and drinks. All this is a natural expansion and leverage of Nutrition House's inherent core competencies. As they say, "Better Health Lives Here".

Our mission is to 'Lead and Foster Well-Being Responsibly.' As such, education plays a large role in our organization. We feel it's important to not just sell products, but to provide natural health solutions. These include lifestyle changes, proper nutrition through diet and supplementation, exercise, and rest.

Wayne Parent, President, Nutrition House

Industrial companies too

A manufacturer perceived themselves as being in the business of making and distributing bottles and caps for consumer and industrial products—until they moved to rethinking the benefits they provide to their end-users. First, they realized that they weren't selling plastic components; they were selling new possibilities for their customers, possibilities that made their lives better and easier. They became co-visionaries with their clients, enhancing their growth potential as well as its own.

Now their communications material speaks in the language of their client and focuses on the benefits they bring to making their lives better. Consequently, communications imagery moved away from a product-centric view of empty bottles and caps to showing the consumer products that their bottles and caps became when decorated and put on shelf.

It's not about size

As you can see from these examples, you don't have to be a multinational company (i.e., Disney, Apple) to understand and apply the principles in this book. In fact, it is often easier if you are a smaller, more flexible, entrepreneurial-minded group. In larger companies it is sometimes more effectively done by starting within a business unit, division or even a large department.

Remember, this exploratory step is about kick-starting an entrepreneurial and customer-centric mindset and one of the guiding principles is: *If you are not going to change customers' lives, stay in bed*.

Everybody can explore

Customer-centric thinking is never limited, every product or service can make a difference in the lives of customers. Just ask the people who brought you California Raisins, Sunkist oranges or Chiquita bananas. People didn't simply buy them to eat fruit; they chose them because they had been branded as natural and fun. Remember how the raisin industry repositioned raisins as "Nature's candy?" Don't tell me that that didn't impact millions of parents who were trying to convince their kids to eat fruit instead of candy.

Once you can get your people to move beyond the traditional product-centric thinking, you have a chance to build brand equity. So after you have established a customer-centric hypothesis, you can begin to build a more relevant brand—testing it against your customers and the competition and honing a positioning statement that resonates in your customers' lives.

Not every company is going to put a man on the moon, but the ones that understand themselves and the market are the ones that can change peoples' lives. They are the ones that grow. Did Apple change its customers' lives? Did Disney? Revlon? Home Hardware? Rock Wood? You bet they did—and they continue to do so. Are you next?

— Tencer and Cardoso

Chapter

10

●

Step Three
Building a relevant brand

What is a relevant brand? It's always relevant to your customers. It delivers what the customers want in a way that is compelling and clearly differentiated from your competition. Whether you are building a company or selling a product or service, they should all be branded to ensure they find a relevant and lucrative market.

When it comes to creating and sustaining a successful brand, it's easier to fail than succeed. The market dumpsters are full of brands that may have started out with a chance to win, but lost their way and became irrelevant. The *90% Rule* model not only helps you build your brand, it ensures that you continue to strengthen its relevance in the marketplace.

Getting it right and keeping it relevant

This chapter focuses on the components of a relevant brand and brings structure to building a sustainable brand. Its purpose is to help you know how to:

What is a relevant brand? It's always relevant to your customers. It delivers what the customers want in a way that is compelling and clearly differentiated from your competition. Whether you are building a company or selling a product or service, they should all be branded to ensure they find a relevant and lucrative market.

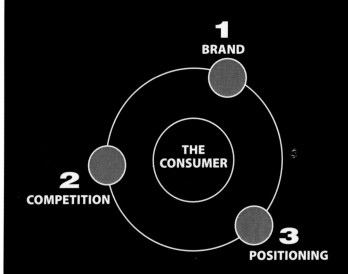

- Define your brand
- Determine what makes it relevant to your most financially significant customer groups
- Develop the most effective ways to communicate those benefits so that they are perceived to be different from other products and services in your category
- Ensure that your brand remains relevant

Too many companies think they understand their brand when, in fact, they don't. When we apply our model, they are surprised at how "off" their understanding has become. Too many assumptions, too little vigilance.

You can get fame quickly. But building a brand with real depth is no quick fix.

Carl Lyons, Marketing Director, lastminute.com

There are many factors that undermine the chance of a brand succeeding. Some are so obvious that I have trouble understanding why companies allow them to happen.

- Not clearly defining the brand and aligning it with the company's strengths, thereby never being able to deliver the "brand promise." Example: Many companies try to brand themselves as low-cost providers, but they can't consistently compete with the big guys (i.e., Wal-Mart, Costco) who can be, and are, the low-cost leaders.
- Not tracking consumer trends, needs and wants and adapting and refining the brand accordingly.
- Not taking the time to understand customers' specific wants and needs so as to ensure that the brand is continually accepted in the marketplace.
- Not taking the time to do a comprehensive competitive survey to understand the different ways in which

customers can satisfy their needs through competitive products and services—unless you plan to be a "me too" provider.

It's not about you

I don't think I can ever say this enough: "It's not about you." I am always amazed at how disconnected a company can get from this fundamental premise. You don't buy what you make; you make the product to sell to other people, so their vote counts the most. Whatever you produce, it is for someone else, so your brand better be relevant to that someone.

> *There is only one boss; the customer. And he can fire everybody in the company from the chairman on down, simply by spending his money somewhere else.*
>
> Sam Walton, founder, Wal-Mart

Customer-centric, not egocentric

It is very easy to put you and the company and your product or service at the centre of your thinking because it's "where you live." It is what you do and know best. But you and all your "stuff" are not all-important. What's important—the elephant in the room (smack-dab in the middle of your planning and operation)—is the customer who, too often, is ignored. This is why the customer, not you, stands at the center of our *90% Rule* model. Because customer needs should drive every decision you make.

Understanding what your customers want requires constant vigilance. After all, their needs and wants change constantly and if your brand is to be relevant it must adapt so you need to track the customer continually. Our model ingrains such a process into your operation.

I don't think I can ever say this enough: "It's not about you." You don't buy what you make; you make the product to sell to other people, so their vote counts the most.

Our strategic principle

20% of a strategic decision is impacted by your company and industry insights; 20% by the professional experience that we bring to the work; and 60% by the customer's voice. That 60% can make or break you. Only when you begin to really understand your customers and their wants and needs can you begin to build a successful brand and sustainable business.

Whatever the customer wants

I was once on a conference call to help stage the re-launch of a national store brand for a leading retail chain. Because the client's products often required explanation to the shopper, a member of the chain's merchandising team asked if they should set up the specific section to suit the needs of the store owners or the in-store shopping patterns of the customer. One of the store owners piped in to say, "Set up the section to the liking of the customer, and I'll adapt." He has it right. This is an example of day-to-day "right thinking." Think like the customer. Think like the customer. Think like the customer.

Question: Do you constantly think like the customer and adapt accordingly?

The idea is to befriend your customer and get to know not only what he and she wants, but what they might need in the future. Quite often, the important things that you learn are subtle, which is why you need a systematic means of capturing new information and ideas.

Henry Ford once said, "If I had asked my customers what they wanted, they would have told me a better buggy whip." Well, Mr. Ford didn't give them a new improved buggy whip, he gave them a quicker, safer and warmer way to travel: a car. I often hear people downplay research by saying, "How can you research something that they (customers) have never seen or don't know about (e.g., a car)? How can they have a valid answer?"

As Marion Plunkett of Plunkett Communications Inc. explains, research can help you to identify problems that customers are having with products or services that are currently available to them in the marketplace. They might also have suggestions, but it's really up to you to design solutions that work for both customers and the organization. Customers, consumers and users of your product or service can tell you where they are now and where they've been—but not where to go in the future. That's your job. But listening to the "Voice of the Customer"(VOC), helps identify many needs. Here are a few examples of needs-driven solutions to think about:

- A mode of travel to get to the destination faster, safer, dryer and warmer than their old nag Gus. Result? The first Ford.

- A way for vacationers to avoid pulling out their wallets or signing for drinks every five minutes when they're on vacation. Result? The carefree all-inclusive approach to vacations at any level of sophistication you choose: three, four or five stars.

- An easier and less wasteful way of packing school lunches—recognizing that most school-lunch sandwiches are of consistent shape and size—and easier to use than traditional pull, tear and waste plastic wrap. Result? Sandwich bags.

- A way to avoid carrying a "boom box", yet have 5,000 songs with you at any time.
Result? MP3 players and iPods.

The key point here is that research is a way of listening to the consumer identify needs—met or unmet—that can then be translated into new products and services. And customers will always speak in terms of the benefits they are looking for, seldom in terms of specific product features or services.

Research should never be used the way a drunkard uses a lamp post—more for support than illumination.

David Ogilvy, British marketing executive

The most common dismissive reason mentioned for not doing research is, "80% of what research tells us we already knew." Ignore it. It may be true but it misses the point. It's often the next 10% that you weren't sure of that gets confirmed and provides illumination, especially when you do solid information-seeking research. Most importantly, it's the final 10% that you didn't know that is really worthwhile because it can yield critical insights that determine what your customers really need or might need in the future.

The market never lies; it will always tell you what to produce if you listen closely.

Building a brand begins and ends in your customer's mind, not in the products you have to sell.

Brands have always been about the relationship between product and user ... A brand signals a set of expectations and a core understanding that drives everything.

Shelly Lazarus, Chairperson,
Ogilvy & Mather Worldwide, 2000

Relevance lost

Lots of companies develop brands but many can't sustain them. The difference begins with the word "relevant." The brand has either never been relevant to the customer or it lost its relevance along the way—usually because the market and the customer changed and the brand did not. If your brand isn't relevant to what the customer cares about, then the customer isn't going to care about your irrelevant brand. And if you want to be relevant, you had best start with knowing your customer and your market.

The first thing you need to do is to define your brand as you see it today. The good news, that's what you did when you identified your brand's tangible benefits, emotional benefits, personification and brand impact. I don't like to ask people straight out to define their brand because it's a big question and not easy to answer "off the top." So we run those exercises to help define it. As mentioned earlier, a brand is the sum of the tangible, intangible and character traits that you are offering to your customers. Together with the brand impact discussion and development of a brand statement, you are able to define a customer-centric brand and business, which is the essential first step to sustainability. (We'll get back to that exercise in a few pages).

Brand relevance

As I walk through the steps of brand development, please remember that the goal of this book is not to provide a dissertation on branding rather it's to provide three things:

i) A jolt of reality: How the *90% Rule* can play a critical role in the evolutionary growth of your business (of which branding is a part) ii) Entrepreneurial thinking: The kind of thinking that drives innovation, pursues opportunities and leverages current assets (which depend on a strong brand)

iii) A pragmatic process (pictogram): For rethinking, reunderstanding and reaccelerating growth—the elusive next 10% (for which a strong brand is critical)

All that work on benefits helps you get away from product-centric thinking. Whether your shoes come in blue or black is secondary to the emotional and functional benefits and experience that you provide to the customer who wears your shoes. The old adage, "If the shoe fits, wear it," might be more accurately stated in marketing terms as, "If the shoe fits your emotional needs, buy it." First, understand how the benefits obtained from wearing your shoes will help change your customer's life. Yet I am amazed at how many companies I meet whose entire organization operates around a product focus—producing certain colors of shoes because blue sold well last year or black is more efficient to produce. And assuming no one would ever want magenta.

The predominant force in the customer's buying process is based on emotions, not pragmatism. Feelings greatly influence buying decisions and often override logic. Branding is about building a relationship around your customer's key feelings that are relevant to your product/service and company. A brand is experienced by the customer as a set of characteristics and values that they associate with your product or service. Some of those characteristics go to the physical nature, such as your name, logo or wordmark, and others go to the values that a customer perceives or expects to receive from your product or service, or from working with your company. The essence of a brand is essentially determined by visceral and intuitive responses, rather than just practical thinking.

I would say that brilliant architecture transforms the landscape in unique and creative ways, ways that touch us emotionally and intellectually. So too does effective brand architecture, bring together vision, knowledge, experience, needs, benefits and voice that together provide the structure, inspiration and personality that determines a lasting brand.

Brand Architecture®

Great buildings, the ones that leave a lasting impression while serving a functional purpose, begin with a solid blueprint, based on information assembled by the architectural team. In the marketing world we often hear the term "Brand Architecture" (registered Trademark of Plunkett Communications Inc.) and it's an accurate term when properly understood. The dictionary defines an architect as somebody whose job it is to design buildings. That's a little bland for my liking—sort of like calling the Beatles "a band." I would say that brilliant architecture transforms the landscape in unique and creative ways, ways that touch us emotionally and intellectually. So too does effective brand architecture, bring together vision, knowledge, experience, needs, benefits and voice that together provide the structure, inspiration and personality that determines a lasting brand. Every successful brand (product, service or cause) is built on solid and well-defined brand architecture.

Every breath you take

Brand Architecture is designed on the premise that every touch point of a brand is interconnected and needs continuous management. A brand is a living, breathing entity. I often say that every brand architect should have as a theme song the platinum hit by the Police, *Every Breath You Take*[1] (" … every move you make, I'll be watching you"). Because its every move is "watched" and under scrutiny in the marketplace. It must offer authenticity in representation and consistency in delivery. That means never underestimate the importance of every touch point in brand creation, delivery and communications. How your brand looks and performs ("every breath it takes") should be part of your daily thinking.

---

[1] *Every Breath You Take* from 1983 album *Synchronicity* by The Police

Making friends

Like a person, your brand has a personality and make-up that it takes into the marketplace and develops over time. I find it helpful to think of brands in terms of people. We are all born boys or girls, but we grow to become individuals. As individuals, we adopt belief systems that identify how we are going to act in certain situations. We decide what we are going to wear to outwardly express who we are. We choose to eat, drink and exercise (or not). Together, these decisions make us individuals whom others perceive in a certain way and either befriend or not. Think back to your first day of school and how both first impressions and lasting characteristics mattered as you made friends and built relationships. The objective is to develop your brand in such a way that it will make the most friends. If you get it right (and refine it along the way), you will probably have many successful long-term relationships. With over six billion people in the world, you certainly can't befriend everyone. Ditto for the millions of brands looking for their relationship with all those people. But, if you identify and pay attention to the "elephants in the room" (customers) you can become their best friend.

To stretch the friend analogy one more time, it is obvious that popularity counts (backed by good character and value) in gaining friends and building relationships. But do not underestimate how easy it is to lose favor. Customers truly know the value of a friendship—and if your brand is not relevant to their needs then they have little allegiance—and a lot of other choices.

This is critical in both business-to-business and business-to-consumer marketing. The customer is bombarded with choices—there are always options—and in the end they will want to know, and be associated with, the brands (friends) they value the most and believe are most relevant to their life.

Making the ordinary extraordinary: Sketchley Cleaners

Early in my career I had the opportunity to work for one of the pioneers of Canadian advertising, Jerry Goodis. At the time, his work was recognized internationally as creative and built on the principles of branding. And I believe that much of it stands today as relevant, insightful, intrusive and, in many cases, audacious.

One of the more challenging accounts at the agency was the Canadian chain of Sketchley Cleaners. This was at a time in the mid-1980s when we were beginning to realize the enormity of value, "equity," that could be built into a brand. Sure, we had already been witness to decades of products in all categories that had grown and marketed their brand. And Goodis had created his share of memorable brand stories: Wonderbra, Hush Puppies, Canadian Club, Speedy Muffler, Harvey's. But this wave was different. We were seeing commodities such as raisins from California become singing and dancing sensations, and cookies in bright yellow bags with "No Name" become as commonly known as the long time brand-name category leaders. And then came the "No Frills" and "President's Choice" brands (now expanded as far as financial services). The breadth and application of branding fundamentals for an almost endless array of products and services were incredible. And in the midst of this proliferation, the Goodis Agency was faced with branding what was almost universally perceived as a commodity: dry cleaning.

The vision was to create the first uniquely branded chain of dry cleaners in Canada. One that instilled trust and confidence in the consumer—something usually lacking between consumers and a chain of dry cleaners. There were a few individual dry cleaners positioned to offer high quality, but chains were perceived as offering a commodity service.

After extensive examination and defining of what was important to its customers, Sketchley identified a key gap: inconsistent and often poor quality delivered by the cleaner and low expectation of quality in the mind of the consumer. There was a perception that "you got what you paid for." Customers stated that their clothes were important to them, but they had low expectations when it came to how the cleaners treated their clothes. This led to the strategy of Sketchley offering three levels of service, each offering a different combination of quality and price. The customer could choose the price/value they wanted. In turn, this was tied to a positioning statement that emphasized the fact that Sketchley cared about their customers' clothes (they were not a commodity), and that cleaning quality really mattered. Sketchley used their graphic identity symbol of Three Penguins and created three levels of quality (good, better, best) with the positioning line: *We know you love your clothes.* It was the quintessential recognition of the customers' feelings towards their appearance and toward the clothes that they articulated their personal expression. Sketchley's pitch went beyond the customers' clothes to their personal appearance and lifestyle. If a dry cleaning chain could express its recognition of this emotional attachment and imbed it in its brand, then they could differentiate themselves from the competition and build a unique customer-centric relationship and a strong Sketchley brand.

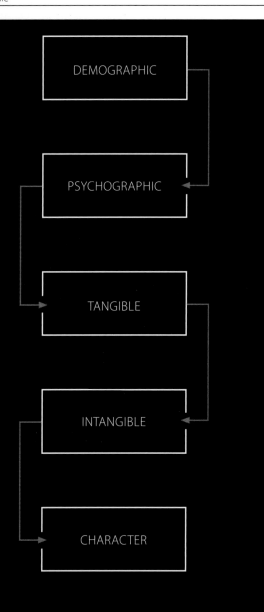

What can your brand be?

Once you have identified the key *tangible* and *emotional* benefits inherent in your products or services and established what business you are in, you have the foundation on which to build a relevant brand.

To confirm that your brand is relevant, we look at three key components:

    I. Customer

    II. Competition

    III. Positioning

I. Customer: Honing in on your most lucrative target groups

You begin by generating a comprehensive list of current and potential target customers, and then identify the ones that you think have the highest and best potential.

Customer identification process, page 110.

Development steps:

1) Using what we call, "life of engagement" is a useful place to start your market analysis to understand current and potential customer groups. This enables you to understand how your customer engages with your company, product or service over the long term. Understanding this behavior makes it easier to hone in on key target markets and segmentation criteria (i.e., demographic and psychographic).

Life engagement examples:

- A toothpaste company understood that to engage customers for life, it needed to reach them from the first time they brushed their teeth. It was first to market with junior toothpaste and children's brushes, and first to offer incremental products (whiteners, floss) at all stages of oral health.

Life engagement:

Toddler → Junior → Teenager → Young Adult → Adult →Senior

- An association engaged in professional development and certification begins reaching people while they are in high school through their introduction to industry. It continues to provide information from continuing education for all to specific services aimed at the executive suite.

Life engagement:

High school → College → Entry → Mid-Mgmt. → Sr. Mgmt → Exec. Suite

2) Delineate your target markets using both demographic and psychographic attributes. To be clear, adults 18-49 who live in Washington, DC is not a sufficient delineation. You must look at and create personifications of your various target groups based on what they like and don't like—all the emotional and practical appeals. What they think, watch, eat, wear, visit, experience, etc. Essentially, we are profiling your customer, just as we did your company.

3) Once you have identified segmentation criteria and target groups, you need to compare what your current and potential customers want in relation to the tangible, intangible and esoteric characteristics that your brand offers. This lets you discuss what it is you are capable of offering to each target and, more importantly, the wants and needs that you are not currently capable of meeting.

NOTE: If you do not have strong customer information, then use this exercise to create a hypothesis about what they want and then confirm your assumptions through qualitative and/or quantitative research.

Before moving on, I want to reiterate point 2). You must go deeper than simply describing where they live or how old they are. Customer profiles must be developed that describe the target group in detail. Think of it this way. If your company is personified as Scrooge, then it probably shouldn't go after customer groups that see themselves as Santa Claus.

II. Competition: Who is else is speaking?

"Oh, we have no real competition" is one of the most dangerous proclamations I have ever heard when it comes to marketing. And I've heard it said so many times, by sober people, that it threatens to drive me to drink (almost).

There is always competition. And if, on a rare occasion, you have no *direct* competition (at that particular moment), you can rest assured you will meet it soon. Many a company has fallen victim to the folly of this "non-competition syndrome." And the smaller the business the more vulnerable you are to this dangerous assumption.

We ignore the competition at our peril.

- Xerox had a brand name so prominent that it became a verb used in every office. When people wanted a copy made they would often say, "Xerox this for me." When the competition struck back, Xerox took decades to recover.

- Aspirin didn't have competition either. You know them, the leading pain-relief medication that has become an afterthought to Advil and Tylenol.

Competition is a given. Believe it.

Now, I don't want this to sound like a knock on the people who said they had no competition because I'm sure they believed it. And in some cases they were probably thinking about direct competition, although I dispute that too. I liken this thinking to the legal concept of conflict of interest. I once asked my lawyer what constituted conflict of interest and he said, "Anything that the other party thinks it is." This may not be the fully articulated legal definition but the point is clear: conflict and competition are often in the mind of the beholder. Except, when it comes to marketing, this non-competition perception will bring the beholder a lot of unwanted conflict. I live by a different assumption: Competition is a given.

The relevant questions should be: What types of competition exist? At what level? Direct or indirect? Now and in the future? Then, of course, you have to think through which of these competitors are most relevant to you. When assessing competition, the first level of questions is fairly straightforward:

- Who do you come across in your daily work life?
- Who are you selling against?
- Who exhibits at the same trade shows as you?
- Who books in to your customers' visitors' logs just before or after you?
- Who has websites that address similar customer needs?

Watching the competition

There is hope for once-leading brands assailed by new competitors.

"Precise as a Swiss watch" is a world-renowned cliché but by the 1980s, the Swiss watch industry was no longer ticking smoothly. Centuries-old craftsmanship was losing ground to cheap Japanese electronics in a market that valued price over tradition. But as industries around the world collapsed in the face of Asian competition, the Swiss watchmakers resolved to save their sector.

Step one was to face facts. To rescue the watch industry, so essential to Switzerland's international reputation, old-time craftsmanship was no longer enough. In the face of foreign competition, Swiss watchmakers would have to become more efficient, competitive, and market-savvy.

The revolution began with consultant Nicolas Hayek, who engineered the 1983 merger of two troubled giants, ASUAG (which included the Longines and Rado brands) and SSIH (makers of Omega and Tissot) into one company known as SMH. Hayek demanded that the new company retool to develop cheaper modular components and invest in more stylish design to combat the low labor costs of overseas producers.

The result was the Swatch, which originally meant "Second Watch," and is now understood to mean "Swiss watch," showing how successfully the brand has been resurrected. With fun and cheeky stylings, garish plastic components and a $30-$50 price tag, the Swatch gave consumers an affordable alternative to Seiko and other Japanese manufacturers. Inside, the quartz watch had been reinvented with new materials and assembly technology, reducing the number of components from 91 to 51—and slashing production costs by 80%.

By 1986, SMH was recognized as the world's leading watchmaker and Hayek had taken control of the company as chairman and CEO. By emphasizing new technology, production innovation and design, and employing marketing alliances with leading international designers, Swatch's analog watches have held their own in a digital world.

Today, the Swatch brand includes children's models, ultra-thin and Scuba watches, metal and plastic watches, seasonally-themed products and even Swatch jewelry. Recognizing the power of the brand it had created, SMH renamed itself Swatch Group in 1998. Yet it still markets most of the world's most high-end watch brands, including Breguet, Blancpain, Glashütte Original, Omega, Certina, Mido and Calvin Klein.

Today, Swatch's manufacturing innovations show up in everything from telecommunications to microelectronics—and even in the modular assembly of Daimler AG's Smart Car, a project actually launched by Swatch. The company's success against all odds proves that when a company pools its expertise with the latest technology and a passion for marketing, new opportunities are not just possible, but abundant.

Hang out with the competition

If you haven't recently done it, now is the time to find out everything you can about your competition. And it is easy to get started, right in your own office. The power of observation can produce informational gems. The best way to take a closer look at your competition is to bring them into your office and let them hang out for a while. Put them up on your wall literally. Pin up their ads, brochures, web pages, mission statements, product samples, price lists, locations and any other intelligence you can find. Then stare at them for a while. You will be amazed at what you can learn if you make an objective assessment of what you see.

Competitive overview process

Your assessment of the competition can start simply by evaluating (on a scale of 1 to 10) what you and your team think of their overall company, their key points and their products/services. Be honest. Leave your ego at the door.

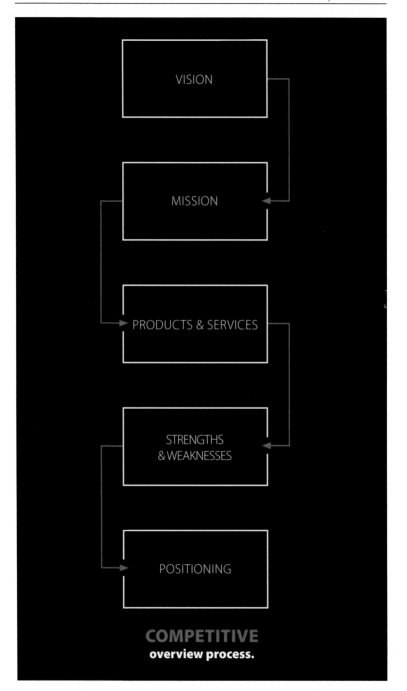

- What is their image, their voice or their brand—or lack thereof?

- Do they identify their vision and mission? Does it make an impression?

- Who are they speaking to?

- How do they talk about their products and services?

- How is their overall presentation, look and message?

- Do they have a brand? Is it strong, weak, consistent or non-existent?

- Are their key messages strong, average, weak or even valid?

- What do they say about their competition (you), directly or implied?

- How do their key points compare to yours?

- How do you perceive them to be positioned?

- How well do they tell their story and make their case?

- Where do you think they are missing the boat?

- Most importantly, what can you say or do that is both relevant and different—from the customers' perspective?

At the end of this process, formalize your findings. Create a *Competition Overview* that compiles the information about your own company and what you know about the competitors. You will note that the last point on the list, Positioning, is the next thing that you have to work on.

After your in-office analysis, and as part of building your brand architecture, you can do a more in-depth analysis of the competition (i.e., customer interviews, focus groups, quantitative research, etc.).

How do you stack up?

Don't ever get tired of asking: "What it is that I am offering that is different from my competition and will change my customers' lives?"

Not to pick on one specific industry sector, but manufacturers pretty much make the top of the heap when it comes to presenting what they think is important (*features*) versus the most relevant customer *benefits*. In their brochures, they love to feature beauty shot after beauty shot of their products. They often lead with close-ups and specifications. They seem to ignore the fact that what they are manufacturing usually looks frighteningly like what their competitors make. Then there's the obligatory plant tour shots. Let's be real for a minute. If you produce millions of widgets a year and sell them to a host of Fortune 500 companies and you are also ISO certified, it is safe to say that people who are contacting you assume that you have a plant somewhere; one that is probably pretty big and reasonably well run. So unless you are the only one in your industry with a plant that makes a product, you can probably keep its picture off the front of your brochure—and off the back page, too. None of this does anything to make your brand relevant.

Where is your point of differentiation? What can you do or say to set your product apart? Because people are busy today, and every day, so you'd better be making a first impression that connects rather than just looking like another ripple in the ocean. Otherwise, you might just as well stay in bed because not only is your brand irrelevant, it doesn't exist in the mind of your customers.

I understand that it is important for manufacturers to provide technical specifications and to show that they are equal to the competition, but ad nauseam is not relevant. These seemingly minor mistakes can kill a brand before it is born and not understanding all the little things that aggregate into creating a memorable brand can prevent you from ever making a lasting impression in customers' minds. It can undermine your position in the market and lead to the demise of your brand, even your business.

Little things make a difference

First, let's remember the old saying, "Little things can make a big difference." We all have examples from our own experience of the little things that make us loyal to certain stores, products and services. Or make us never go back. One such example for me is my cellular provider. I am sure you remember how phone companies locked you into long-term contracts and rates that would remain high with no relief unless you paid a penalty to get out of the contract, usually by switching providers. Where is the benefit to the business in that? Make a little more in the short term but lose the customer forever after only a year or two. It's no wonder that providers were constantly churning customers. But my service provider has managed to keep me for many years now. Why? Because I get calls on a fairly regular basis from their customer care department. They say that they have been monitoring the use of my business' phones over the last few months and have found a less expensive monthly package for me and if I agree to it today they will discount the overages from the previous month. That is an excellent customer-centric benefit and in return I am a loyal, long-term customer. Another customer-centric business is any restaurant that deletes a charge from my bill with no questions asked when I have had any sort of problem with the food or service. The result? I'll come back— in part to return the respect they showed me.

The *90% Rule* is based on operating leverage as a marketing tool and the requisite cornerstone for maximizing leverage is the strength of your brand and that strength has a great deal to do with how you position it against the competition.

III. Positioning: If it isn't relevant and memorable, it's lost

In their landmark book, *Positioning: The Battle for Your Mind*, Al Ries and Jack Trout explained positioning this way: "To succeed in our over-communicated society, a company must create a position in the prospect's mind. A position that takes into consideration not only a company's strengths and weaknesses, but those of its competitors as well"[2]. Sketchley did exactly this.

The focus on customer thinking needs to be converted into your brand positioning by pursuing the main question: *What can your brand be that is most relevant to the customer and clearly differentiates it from what is already available in the market?* Always look for options that you believe your organization has the capability of building, delivering, servicing and embodying. These options form a hypothesis and provide a test platform for determining which brand concept can win the most friends and influence the most people. Here are a few obvious examples of questions that help define your brand options:

- Most exclusive brand or a brand for the masses?
- Safest car or most stylish?
- Freshest and fastest to market or biggest selection?
- Full service or self-serve?
- Carefree and light, or serious?
- Top of the line and as good as the best for a little less?
- Long-lasting or less durable and less costly?
- Brand leader or generic substitute?

This part of the process helps you figure out and bring together the two sides of the equation: What the consumer

[2] *Positioning: The Battle for Your Mind*, Al Ries and Jack Trout, page 29

will want, perceive, experience, believe and always gravitate toward. And what you can deliver on, profitably.

Positioning and branding are inextricable. A positioning statement links both what the customer needs and the benefits you offer and the brand must create that positioning in the minds of your customers. Positioning evolves from the process of exploring, rethinking and redefining and rises like cream to the surface as you stir and remix the collective thinking about your business and brand.

Nothing expresses a brand better than a successful positioning exercise translated into a memorable positioning slogan. We all remember our favorites and the good ones transcend time:

"We try harder" (Avis)

"A Kodak moment" (Kodak)

"It's the real thing" (Coca Cola)

"At Speedy you're a somebody" (Speedy Auto Services)

"We know you love your clothes" (Sketchley Cleaners)

"… we care about the shape you're in" (Wonderbra)

"Just slightly ahead of our time" (Panasonic)

"I Love New York" (New York State)

"The Ultimate Driving Experience" (BMW)

"Technology you can enjoy" (Honda)

"I am Canadian" (Molson Canadian)

"I'm lovin' it" (McDonalds)

"Have it your way" (Burger King)

"Harvey's makes a hamburger a beautiful thing" (Harvey's)

"Real women have real curves" (Dove)

"Because you're worth it" (L'Oreal)

"Because owners care" (Westjet Airlines)

"Buy Canadian, the rest of the world does" (Canadian Club)

"The man in the Hathaway shirt" (Hathaway Shirts)

"Think small" (Volkswagen)

You don't have to be an international brand to have an effective positioning and slogan. One of the more memorable slogans that I've heard is for a Toronto-based plumbing contractor, Roto-Rooter: "Number one in the number two business."

Going back over what a few of my favorite marketing authors and speakers have said, I have paraphrased the essence of why positioning is so important.

> *If you offer the same thing as your competitor for the same amount of money backed by the same level of service, chances are you are pretty much the same as everybody else and you're not going to be winning much new business. It may seem obvious but let's face it, not every company in a sector can have the best people, best engineering, best service, best product, best price and offer the best same thing. That's not reality. Reality is, every product or service has to carve out a recognizable position for itself in the minds of the consumers, and then fight like hell to maintain and strengthen it.*

Determine positioning, then make a statement

Do not confuse positioning points with a positioning slogan. Both are essential but points are singular ideas that communicate where you want to be in the customer's mind. They precede the slogan. The slogan drives home your positioning in a creative and memorable way.

Brand → positioning point(s) → positioning slogan

Here are examples of slogans created from, and built on, strong positioning that we are all familiar with:

- Lever 2000 soap → cleansing, deodorizing and moisturizing →

For all your body parts

- Southwest Airlines → less for much less →

We give people the freedom to fly

- BMW → performance →

The ultimate driving experience

- Coke → always first → number one →

The real thing

- Barack Obama → change needed → desire for change→ hope →

Yes we can!

Most of our clients have worked through this process—including our own company—and the results are always a better, more compelling positioning. Here are a few brief sketches of the thinking that produced successful new positioning insights.

Angus Systems

With an influx of upstart dot-com companies offering property-management software in the commercial real estate sector, Angus Systems came to Spyder Works to help them "remind" the market that it had been in property management for eighty-five years and knew the business first-hand.

Explains Chris Gale, CEO of Angus Systems, "It was critical for us to create marketing messaging that embraced our history of industry leadership and clearly differentiated us from our dot-com competitors."

Devising a new corporate message, brand identity and client-focused story, we used a case history approach to demonstrate that Angus understood the nuts and bolts of its clients' business and had seamless solutions that fit with their existing processes.

Angus' parent company began over 85 years ago as a consulting engineering firm that designed mechanical and electrical systems. The firm's growth and success over the next 40 years led to a significant number of clients asking Angus to run and maintain the building systems that its engineering group designed. Then, after more than 20 years of working for property managers, maintaining their building systems, the company created Angus Systems to develop purpose-built service and maintenance management software for commercial real estate.

Since the inception of Angus Systems, the company has maintained a relentless commitment to innovation. The launch of their latest version of Angus AnyWhere™ marks their tenth generation of software, and the culmination of literally hundreds of updates. Angus has pioneered web enablement and wireless capability for their software system to ensure that their customers can access Angus AnyWhere™ easily, from anywhere.

Today, their software supports more than one billion square feet of commercial real estate across North America in buildings from 20,000 square feet to portfolios of more than 100 million square feet. It capitalizes on the internet and wireless technologies to provide a structured and streamlined workflow to put building owners, property managers, tenants, staff and vendors on the same page.

Buildings are the company's heritage. As "someone" once said, "To help predict the future, you should look to the past."

Angus Systems: Buildings are our heritage™

Spyder Works

At Spyder Works we went through the same process of asking ourselves, what can we do to position ourselves differently? And, of course, we found that the bulk of the answer came from our customers.

As we explored our accumulation of years building different businesses and working with clients to help them build businesses, we found what one client called our "sweet spot." We dug a little deeper.

We hung a lot of our competitors up on the office wall and realized that most of those in our space came at it either with a big company positioning (usually experience-based at the top and under-experienced below) or as a single-source solution (specialized consulting in research or strategic planning or design or advertising or interactive).

We learned from our customers (ranging from those building their own businesses to those responsible for divisions of large companies) that what they wanted and needed most was a "partner" with a handful of critical attributes:

- A hands-on group who bring to the table relevant, senior business thinking that is immediately applicable

- A group that has the capacity to provide both the up front planning and thinking as well as the ongoing implementation services (product, price, distribution, branding and across-the-board communications)

- A flexible group that adapts to the specific needs—both immediate ("fire fighting") and longer-term (sustainable growth)

- A fully engaged extension of the management team

- A group that provides senior expertise and insight into pressing go/no-go decision points in the organization's business development
- A group that although a temporary part of the team, makes sure that the new, collective thinking sticks long after they have left (install a systematic process)
- A group that delivers on time and on budget
- A group that is affordable on a cost/value basis and helps get the most out of what we are already good at

Our customers needed a range of in-depth, experienced thinking that directly related to specific decision-making and ongoing action. It was obvious they needed "plug-in partners" who could bring to them additional new, objective and innovative *thinking and doing*. As simple as it sounds, we boiled it down to the fact that our customers wanted and needed us to help them "think" and "do" a number of very specialized things.

We recognized their exasperation with the break between strategic thinking and design, branding and the execution of communications. Clients were used to hiring two or three firms to help solve a wide range of problems, which forced them to act as a bridge between firms in areas were they did not have the in-house expertise (e.g. research, strategy, design, communications). Consequently, there was no seamless connection between the thinking and the execution, which produced inconsistent strategies, weak branding and sub-par communications.

So we positioned ourselves as "partners" who bring to our clients a step-by-step process that helps them refine their growth plans and develop innovative strategies, integrated design and a relevant brand that embodies the company across all internal and external communications. This thinking is the cornerstone of the *90% Rule*™ (a strategic process that leads to tactical implementation), and our trademarked model, *Building Business by Design*™.

Not only does the positioning work, it differentiates us in the marketplace. And most importantly, we provide the client with a built-in, sustainable process that ties the market directly to goals, strategies, brand and communications. And leverage it for sustainable growth.

I've received a very salient compliment from a long-time client who had worked with many consultants and agencies. She said, "I like working with you guys because there's no fluff."

IV. Pricing strategy

As we have seen, there are many different ways to differentiate your company and its products or services from the competition; however, everyone seems to start at the same place: price. I don't recommend it and this mistake needs to be addressed by almost every company.

The important thing to realize is that price is most often employed as a tactic but mistakenly talked about as a strategy. Why? Primarily because we tend to ignore value *as perceived by the customer*, which we do because we have not taken a customer-centric view in the first place. When our thinking is product-centric, we tend to focus on cost and set the price primarily based on costs rather than understanding the inherent value from the customer's perspective. We set price according to their values, which in turn, should be part of our overall growth strategy (as identified from our best opportunities). This makes price a strategic decision.

If your best opportunities are in the higher end of the market then quality and pricing become a critical part of strategy and part of the value you want your brand to reflect. It is not a tactical add-on. Price by itself—as in "cheaper"—is not enough; there must be clear benefits layered into what you offer. As we all know, strong branding can achieve premium pricing (Heinz, Sony, Monteblanc, Whirlpool) and premium pricing can complement and strengthen branding.

Price and pricing strategies are a balancing act between cost (what it costs to produce and deliver) and value (what customers perceive and are willing to pay). How much is too much? How much is not enough? Your pricing is the proverbial moving target that you must strategically determine and then continually monitor and manage.

The adage, "You get what you pay for" may be old but it certainly isn't tired. I have never wanted to be the lowest-price supplier at anything that I do, even when I manufactured commodities. And certainly not when proposing to help other people build value. Let's face it, there can be only one lowest-cost supplier and all other competitors are positioned somewhere else. Or they die trying to be what they can't be. Case in point: in mass-market retail, Wal-Mart and Costco are the only companies that can maintain price leadership positions. Everyone else needs a different pricing strategy and one that works in close concert with their positioning (e.g., Target, Walgreens, Zellers, The Bay).

When you have a clear positioning you need to connect a clear pricing strategy to it because positioning and price are inextricably linked.

Final check

Scour your history, especially the emotional history, and look for "gems." Then look at it through the customer's eyes and talk to them. They can share invaluable knowledge that will help anchor your positioning statement. What satisfied customers say about you, in their own words, can be a springboard to defining your positioning in a new, more customer-centric way.

Creating and sustaining a relevant brand is critical to sustainable growth. Without it, your brand will always be an afterthought in customers' minds—if it's thought of at all. Define it, create it, position it, price it, maintain it.

— *Tencer and Cardoso*

Chapter

Step Four
Leveraging with
the *90% Rule*™

... the essence of strategic reasoning is the ability to creatively challenge "the tyranny of the given" (Kao, 1996) and to generate new and unique ways of understanding and doing things.

De Wit and Meyer, authors, Strategy Synthesis

It's worth repeating. Entrepreneurial thinking assumes that there is never a shortage of opportunities, only a perceived shortage of resources. And that if you do your due diligence to identify your best opportunities, as well as the strength of the resources you *already* have, you will uncover all the leverage power you need. If there is one thing I want you to take away from this book, it is the fact that your business can benefit far more from a growth strategy built on *leveraging relevant opportunities* than it can from ever-changing strategies and tactics based on short-term performance and chasing fragmented growth and hope.

The application of the *90% Rule* gives you two fundamental benefits:

If there is one thing I want you to take away from this book, it is the fact that your business can benefit far more from a growth strategy built on *leveraging relevant opportunities* than it can from ever-changing strategies and tactics based on short-term performance and chasing fragmented growth and hope.

i) It creates a clear and essential context in which you can make strategic decisions (steps one, two, three)

ii) It allows you to identify your best opportunities and leverage your current assets against them

He who pursues many things accomplishes nothing.

Anonymous

Defining opportunity

There is no dearth of opportunities; they are everywhere. The key is in clearly defining the few that are most relevant for you. For that, we like creating our own relevant definitions and at this stage in the process, we define business opportunity as:

"A set of circumstances that makes it possible to accomplish something *that is actionable and measurable.*"

First, you need to evaluate and organize potential opportunities into highest-and-best-return groups and identify *what you are leveraging, against what, and for what purpose.* I call these the 3Ws of leveraging: *What. What. What.*

Leverage dictates that you identify:

1) What are you leveraging?

What you are leveraging could be any of a number of assets, values or capabilities. If you're good at quality, leverage it more. If you're good at new product development, do more of it. If you're good at time-to-market, leverage it more. If you're good at customer service, get even better. If your current brand is not strong enough, make it stronger. And if it is strong, communicate that message better.

2) Against what?

If you've identified your customer-driven benefits then you will get your best leverage by working on the capabilities/assets that best match the needs of your key customer groups and differentiate you from your competition. There's no point leveraging something you're good at if it's not high on the customer's list of wanted benefits. And there's no point trying to give the customer something you're not good at and your competition is.

3) For what purpose?

The purpose for all leveraging is to convert opportunities into a more efficient return on the investment (ROI) you have in your core assets (defined and measured specifically). Do this by delivering the specific benefits your customers want. And make sure you identify where this ROI is and how it can be measured.

If you leverage the wrong things to the wrong customers, or against the wrong benefits, you will get the wrong results. This step is designed to help you find the optimum points of leverage by refining a full range of opportunities down into a manageable and best-return group. Each business is different and we have had clients start with more than fifty "blue sky" opportunities and then build a plan around as few as two. Others have ended up with as many as eighteen.

Converging opportunities

We call this part of the process "grounded blue-skying" because you move from generating many blue-sky ideas down to the optimum number of opportunities (See example, Converging Opportunities). You will have identified lots of opportunities when reviewing your history, vision and mission but now the process converges, like a funnel, the many opportunities into a few. You end up with specific measurable opportunities that you can pursue based on who you are targeting, what you believe they want and what you are 90% capable of delivering.

Spyder Works

Step 1: From our broad vision, mission and goal we determined more than fifty opportunities for growth, all around cultivating entrepreneurial thinking in companies of all sizes.

Step 2: Our overall target focus was on businesses and/or divisions between $20—$200 million with goal of double-digit growth. And organizations needing what we were already capable of offering (integrated services).

Step 3: Matched specific products/service benefits to highest and best potential customer needs based on assessment of four leveraging questions.

Step 4: Leveraged assets, particularly the intellectual capital invested in one-to-one engagements by: a) Finding new clients as natural extension of current base; and b) creating a one-to-many platform that offers more services beyond and/or in conjunction with regular consulting— seminars, books and discussion networks.

Step 5: Evaluated opportunities against three key criteria: Opportunity to expand internationally, specifically U.S.A.; add some short selling cycle services to complement longer cycles and form strategic alliances; improve financial performance (revenue, cash flow, margins) with little additional investment.

CONVERGING
opportunities.

Highest-and-best-return

In this step, you create an *Opportunity Assessment* (see *Opportunity Assessment*) by brainstorming all the opportunities that are in keeping with your overall vision and mission and focused on your core markets. The brainstorming is guided by three broad factors (see below: global, market, financial) and four key marketing questions, which are founded on the same analytical principles of Ansoff's matrix[3] and other similar tools and models.

Four leveraging questions

All your blue sky opportunities need the following overarching questions applied to them during the process of convergence.

#1: Market Penetration

What can you do to *increase sales to existing customers* in existing markets with existing products?

Examples:

- Use of baking soda in a refrigerator
- Serving eggs for dinner
- New stores in current markets—improve accessibility
- Improvements in pricing

#2: Market Development

What can you do to develop *new sales in existing markets by attracting new customers?*

Match current products and services to "fence sitters" and new prospects. Consider any adjacent or incremental opportunities that emerge from your analysis.

---

[3] Ansoff, Igor (1957), "Strategies for Diversification", *Harvard Business Review,* 35(5), September-October, 113-124. Examples were also adapted from Papadopoulos, Nicolas, William Zikmund, and Michael D'Amico (1988), *Marketing* (Toronto, ON: John Wiley & Sons Canada), Ch. 9

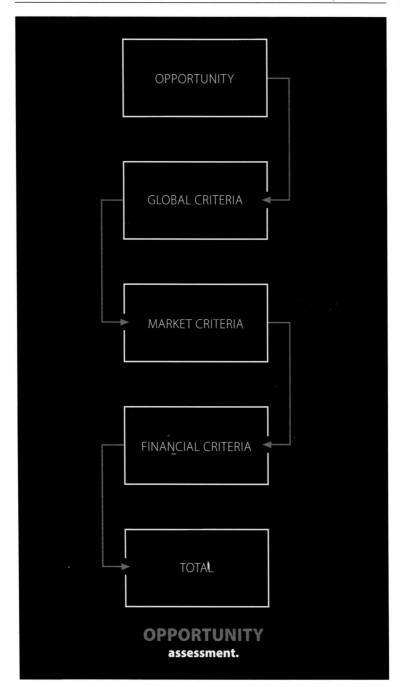

Examples:

- Running shoes marketed as walking shoes to seniors
- PCs to the high-school market
- McDonald's expands hours by offering breakfast and coffee
- Tim Hortons goes beyond doughnuts and adds sandwiches

#3: Product Development

What can you do to *increase sales to existing customers in existing markets with new products?*

Develop and offer modified or new products to current markets.

Examples:

- Salads at fast-food restaurants
- Seminars and "lunch and learns," instead of full-length courses
- Professional sports teams selling branded clothing

#4: Product Diversification

What can you do to *increase sales to new customers in new markets with new products?*

Product diversification by marketing new products to current and new customers.

Examples:

- Introduction of Gap Adventures
- Starbucks purchase of music company Hear Music to play and sell CDs in stores
- Apple Computer introduces the iPod
- Spyder Works develops seminars, books, online products and services

Prioritizing

- Generate an extensive list of opportunities that you can offer based on who you are targeting and what the customer wants.

- Rank and assign five stars to the opportunities believed most relevant, then four stars, three, and so on

- Next list the top ten opportunities as identified by star allocation

As you identify and rank opportunities according to the star allocation also rank them according to these three categories:

Global factors:

- In-keeping with your vision
- In-keeping with your mission
- In-keeping with positioning
- Your "gut check" (intuition)

Market factors:

- Length of the selling cycle
- Potential for long-term growth
- Customer and market group
- Potential competition
- Expertise
- Time to market

Financial factors:

- Impact on revenue
- Impact on cash flow
- Margin contribution
- Required investment (low requirement is 10)
- Required personnel (low requirement is 10)

Once you have matched the opportunities to your strategies, you can transform strategy into tactical action. Then you're ready to put together a go-to-market plan of action.

Top ten

By the end of the *Opportunity Assessment* you want to arrive at the "top ten" best opportunities (give or take a couple). And then there is one more step: The top three (give or take). These are always custom-tailored to your particular needs and situation and whether you have two or ten, each opportunity must be anchored in the principles of the *90% Rule*—it is your highest and best potential for growth and it can be highly leveraged with your current assets.

A cautionary trail

The path between strategic and tactical thinking is filled with bumps and excuses, particularly the established, encrusted, assumptive and subjective ones that rationalize why old opportunities are better than new ones. We know it takes a tough objective assessment—the key word being objective—to boil many opportunities down into a handful of the best. Too often, companies have convoluted reasons for hanging on to some customers and chasing old opportunities—for all the wrong reasons. For example:

- Has been a customer for 100 years
- Generates high sales volume (unspoken, low margin)
- Is a favorite customer (usually based on personally preferred relationship, not business)
- Can't afford to lose the cash flow
- They're a subsidiary of our biggest customer

If the ranking of opportunities is not done thoroughly and matched to your strategy and current capabilities, you will have little chance of converting even the best of strategies into effective, highly leveraged, tactical execution.

> *The strength of the 90% Rule is leverage. The strength of the leverage lies in matching your current resources to the best opportunities, and then driven by the best possible strategies that can turn actionable and measurable opportunities into bottom line results and sustainable growth.*
>
> — *Tencer and Cardoso*

Chapter

12

■

Step Five
Mapping your opportunities:
The Opportunity Matrix

The great discoveries are usually obvious.

Philip Crosby, author of Quality is Free

Entrepreneurs do not walk in lockstep with conventional wisdom or follow traditional maps; they chart their own course (just ask Christopher Columbus). If you intend to have a say in shaping your future, it's important to understand how to shape what you offer so that it best fits the map of the marketplace.

Mapping opportunity

The *Opportunity Matrix* enables you to assess the work that you have done to date. You began by working through your high-level opportunities right down to your actionable, measurable ones. Now it's important to build consensus and cross-disciplinary team "buy-in" by including a full complement of people in the process of assessing, contributing and allocating internal resources to the new opportunities.

Opportunities don't come to fruition because of the work of a few people. The exercise of plotting the top opportunities

Opportunities don't come to fruition because of the work of a few people. The exercise of plotting the top opportunities brings together knowledge and thinking from all functions of your company. What teams will your opportunities require? HR? Engineering? R&D? Marketing? Sales? Manufacturing? Finance? All of the above?

brings together knowledge and thinking from all functions of your company. What teams will your opportunities require? HR? Engineering? R&D? Marketing? Sales? Manufacturing? Finance? All of the above? These discussions identify the strength of available resources and how best to allocate them. For example, if the majority of opportunities are short-term and dependent on human capital, it raises the question of whether you have the people in place to achieve your objectives. Conversely, if many of the opportunities are in the long-term, it means looking at longer-term financial options.

The one thing that many people forget to ask during the strategic process is: What are we going to need to get this done?

Opportunity Matrix

Your go-to-market resource requirements and considerations are linked to the quadrants on the matrix. Within the Opportunity Matrix are:

- **Quadrant 1:** Short-term implementation based on financial capital
- **Quadrant 2:** Long-term implementation based on financial capital
- **Quadrant 3:** Long-term implementation based on human capital
- **Quadrant 4:** Short-term implementation based on human capital

If all the opportunities you have identified rank in the top-right quadrant, then developing all these opportunities will take a lot of money and time. So what are you going to do for the next three years? Conversely, if everything is in the top-left quadrant then you need a lot of money and everything needs

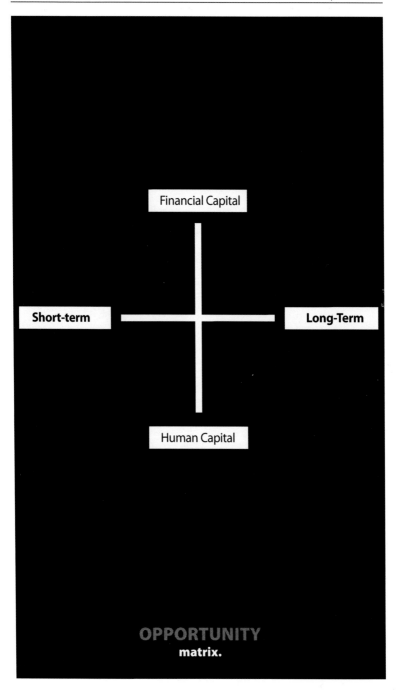

to be done tomorrow. The same analogies can be drawn for the quadrants that relate to the need for capital.

You can't build a building in bits and pieces, but you can build a complex one building at a time. It's time to be resourceful.

The goal is to come up with a manageable flow of opportunities. So if you find that too many of your new opportunities are clustering, it's time to drill down deeper and see how you can reconfigure the opportunities and/or break them into stages.

In the list below, notice the word outsourcing and how often it comes up. It may cost a little more in the short-term (i.e., margin), however, it is far less expensive than *building* it yourself—and then find that they don't come.

- A bath and body-care company outsources high-season filling and packaging
- A landscaping company explores interior gardens through outsourcing
- An institute contracts an outside trainer to kick-start its custom-training division
- A bottle manufacturer begins by outsourcing the industrial-design portion of the process due to the lack of full-time need
- A furniture company outsources delivery and installation as demand spikes until the company is sure that the new level of demand is "for real"
- A communications firm began its Web 2.0 practice by subcontracting

My eleventh grade geometry teacher and rugby coach would always yell (loudly) at us, "There are many ways to skin a cat." Excusing the inappropriate metaphor (by today's standards), he was right. Your job is to harness the power of your interdisciplinary team and find the ways, the paths, the steps to achieve what you want with what you have. This is not a time for guesswork or all-or-nothing decision-making. You want to chart your course sensibly but boldly. That takes deliberation and collaboration by everyone involved.

Turning opportunities into projects

Remember, too, it's not just about identifying opportunities but ensuring that they get implemented. Each opportunity can become a project and each project gets a champion. Assign a project leader who is an "opportunity champion" for each project on which you plan to go forward. It is their responsibility to work out the full extent of the opportunity and set out how, when and what it will take to get to market.

Turning opportunity into success

The greater the opportunity, the greater the chance for success.

Marc Eckō: Edge and authenticity

Mark Eckō had a clear map of what he saw in the marketplace. Just as Lacoste has its crocodile and Ralph Lauren has his polo pony, Eckō Unltd. has a rhinoceros as its symbol. To young urban Americans looking for "street cred," the incongruous rhino offers proof positive that they're wearing original Eckō hoodies, jeans, t-shirts or sneakers—the hottest name in casual wear.

Company founder Marc Eckō started his company selling custom spray-painted t-shirts while still a high-school student in Lakewood, New Jersey. By 1993 his colorful graffiti-inspired designs started catching the attention of prominent black hip-hop artists, and Eckō abandoned Rutgers University to sell street clothes full-time. When a line of rhino-themed t-shirts sold out

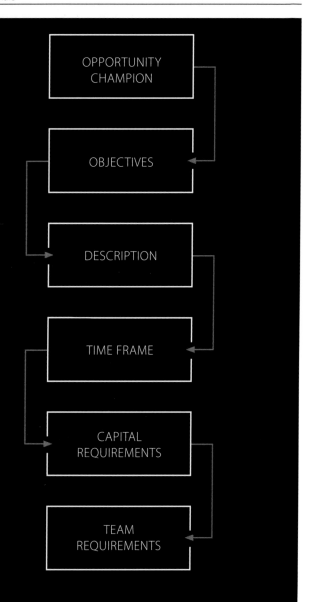

fast, Eckō knew he had found his key visual element. A rhinoceros, you might say, doesn't exactly scream "urban America." But that's the idea. "I think good design makes you scratch your head," says Eckō. "It's the nonlinear bit, the bit that's not logical."

Within three years Eckō had $16 million in sales, but sky-high debt. An angel investor helped the company work down its debt—but his most important contribution was to recognize that Eckō wasn't a t-shirt company, but a lifestyle brand. Switching his focus from creating cool shirt designs to devising radical marketing schemes, Eckō turned the company from a money loser into a lifestyle machine. Eschewing industry fashion shows, for instance, he doubled sales by creating commando teams to sell Eckō clothes right on the street. And he broadened his appeal by expanding into jeans, hoodies and women's and children's fashions with an urban edge.

Today Eckō is an international super-brand, having bought up other edgy brand names such as Zoo York (for the skateboard crowd) and outerwear producer Avirex. The company also produces shoes, hats and watches, and high-end men's fashion "with just the right amount of swagger." There's even a streetwear magazine, Complex, dedicated to spreading Eckō's "community of individuals" culture. Now a billion-dollar company, Eckō has opened its own retail stores to stay in touch with its target market and test new ideas. For instance, controlling its own retail environment helped the company score a big win with (of all things) a high-end line of Star Wars shirts and hoodies. With your own stores, says Marc, you can "do more narrative-based things with the product."

Marc Eckō and his 50% partner, Seth Gerszberg, learned just in time that the "product" is not the brand. By focusing on finding a style and voice for urban youth, they turned the company into a champion of creativity and empowerment.

Today, that quest for authenticity (or "cred") continues. In 2007, Marc Eckō paid $752,467 for the baseball that controversial slugger Barry Bonds hit for his record-breaking 756th home run. He set up a website allowing customers to vote on whether he should donate the ball to the Baseball Hall of Fame in Cooperstown or shoot it into space. The winning idea: send it to the Hall with an asterisk cut into it to acknowledge Bonds' steroid controversy. Eckō's big stunt generated 10 million votes, millions of dollars' worth of free publicity—and cemented his rep as an outlaw with both authenticity and edge.

Implementing strategy

At this point, you have plotted your highest-and-best-potential opportunities, created projects and assigned champions to each. They will refine project implementation strategies that fit with your overall strategy and develop a plan of action. Next, you need to take a look at the most relevant communications and the most effective tools required.

> *Mapping, analyzing and refining opportunities allow you to get beyond the short-term curse of trying to do a whole bunch of things badly, versus a few things really well.*
>
> — *Tencer and Cardoso*

Chapter 13

**Step Six
Speaking to be heard**

If a tree falls in the forest and no one is there, does it make a sound?

Speaking effectively—as in having clear, compelling and consistent communications (strategies, messages and media)—goes a long way to converting your opportunities and sustaining a relevant brand. Too often it is the most underrated and overlooked component of a strategic plan.

The market is a huge, noisy forest. If you expect to survive, you must be there and you must be heard above the din. To do that, you must speak loud and clear and be interesting. Tens of thousands of great products, services and ideas fail because no one notices them or understands their relevance.

Integrating the most effective communications tools allows you to not only carve out a unique position for your brand, but to constantly shape it for the incessantly changing market. If you listen to your customers at each step-to-market, they will tell you if your communications are effective or not.

Matchmaking

All too often people focus on speaking to their end-user, but how about the chain-to-market communications that can create the proverbial broken telephone? If you are able to identify all the people you are speaking to (your communications touch-points), then you have a chance of delivering a consistent, clear message to all of them: Employees, stakeholders, distributors, agents, salespeople ... *and* customers. Only in this way can you create the most effective and efficient communication materials.

Essentially, you need to ensure that you know:

- Who you are speaking to
- What you want to achieve with your communication (e.g. awareness, education, direct response, call to action)
- What action you want to induce (e.g. buy, trial, join, attend)
- How you are most effectively going to reach them

Now you can select the best communications tools based on who you are speaking to and what you want them to do. It's about creating a context for the selection of communication vehicles rather than the all too common practice of going right to the perceived solution (e.g., "We need a Web site," or "a new brochure").

- Describe the chain that your product or service follows from inception to end-use
- Identify what is most important to communicate about your product or service to *each* group in the chain. It can be different (i.e., awareness, information, education, engagement), but it always requires consistency
- Identify the different communications tools in your tool set
- Identify the best tools to reach and engage each group in the chain

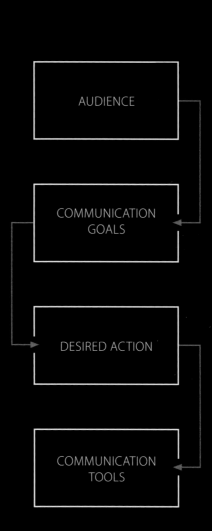

Common communications short-comings

I have found that those companies who do not understand or do not value the power of a strong brand usually make many common mistakes. Here are a few:

- Inconsistency: A company that pins its brand on good customer service and yet has an eight-layer touch-tone phone menu that frustrates consumers trying to get an answer or help. Then they have the gall to insert a voice message that says, "Your call is important to us"—and make you wait five more minutes.

- Misunderstanding of touchpoints: Making decisions based on a flawed understanding of effective communications by thinking, "It's only a fridge magnet, so we can let the printer design it." Except the fridge magnet is the one piece of communication that will live in the customer's home, on its most visible and used appliance, for the longest time. Why would you ever think of minimizing this excellent "Trojan Horse" ambassador?

- Cutting the wrong corners: "The bottle label on the product doesn't have to be more than two colors because it comes in a beautiful box." Oh and, when the box is opened up and thrown away, what lives in the customer's home, representing your brand and reminding the customer of what to buy next time? The bottle, that's right - the one with the poorly conceived label.

- Not utilizing the power of digital and interactive medium to extend brand reach (and increasing these budgets) because they do not understand the "new" media. Or using new media with little or no knowledge of how best to do it.

Marketing is not a series of transactions between a company and its customers; it's about building meaningful, ongoing relationships. The fundamentals of relationship marketing are based on each party not only understanding the tangible benefits they receive from each other, but about creating strong emotional bonds between the brand and its user.

Marketing is not a series of transactions between a company and its customers; it's about building meaningful, ongoing relationships. The fundamentals of relationship marketing are based on each party not only understanding the tangible benefits they receive from each other, but about creating strong emotional bonds between the brand and its user. Building these relationships requires the very best in communications.

The full suite of marketing tools goes beyond traditional advertising or direct mail to create a complete spectrum of benefits:

1. Raise awareness and interest (traditional function of advertising)
2. Provide information and context (long copy print, and Web 1.0 functionality)
3. Induce action (direct response—direct mail, online, interactive)
4. Promote engagement (Web 1.5 functionality)
5. Establish brand advocacy (public relations, Web 2.0 and social media)

This oversimplifies the results you can expect from each tool because you can expect many cross-platform benefits. For example, good advertising can promote engagement and move product, just as social media can raise awareness and sell.

Implementation

Implementation is all about turning marketing into a powerful force and the most effective and efficient way to do that is to understand who you are speaking to, what is important to them and how you want them to react—before trying to establish your communications mix.

Good communications comes from good marketing planning, and good marketing comes from having a clear vision, mission and strategy. All of it focused on converting the best opportunities into the best return on investment.

— *Tencer and Cardoso*

Chapter

14

Step Seven
Success comes from action

Whenever anything is being accomplished, it is being done, I have learned, by a monomaniac with a mission.

Peter Drucker,
American management consultant and author

The *90% Rule* takes you beyond the mythical—sometimes futile—dependency on annual corporate retreats and sporadic seminars to solve your ongoing needs (i.e., more innovation, better opportunities, stronger brand, more sustainable growth). The *90% Rule* gives you a concrete, built-in process anchored to measurable and actionable opportunities that allow you *to get the most out of what you already have.* And it puts innovation on the front burner, every day.

Action-Innovation-Plan (AIP)

If the action is to be consistent, then the process must be integrated into your operations so that the opportunities and priorities are continually front–and–center for everybody

If the action is to be consistent, then the process must be integrated into your operations so that the opportunities and priorities are continually front-and-center for everybody to see, revisit and recalibrate.

to see, revisit and recalibrate. Nothing is more unpredictable than the marketplace and nothing is more elusive than trying to innovate for the market. So it is essential that you provide everyone in your organization with a means to stay on top of what is needed.

1) **Thirty Days:** Meet as a group thirty days after completing the installation of this new process and have each team leader present their project action plan for the identified opportunities.

2) **Innovation Breakouts (monthly):** These are collaborative sessions to review markets and products, exchange ideas, share new thinking and determine how to drive ongoing innovation. From these discussions you revise the action plan as necessary.

3) **Customer Summit (on-site or off):** This is an interactive meeting with your customers to gather feedback and discuss their needs, market trends, industry issues and shared opportunities. These discussions nearly always require you to revise your ongoing action plan.

4) **Annual Summit (on-site or off):** This is a comprehensive evaluation of progress, problems and emerging opportunities. It is also the time to review strategies and resources and recalibrate programs. From these discussions you make revisions to strategies—if any—and readjust tactics accordingly. It's basically a periodic review and refinement of your ongoing process.

These four action steps (AIP) help you integrate the systematic process throughout your organization so that it fuels continuous action, creates widespread innovation and drives sustainable growth.

Plans and opportunities without sustainable and measurable action is like a canoe without a paddle— leaving you, you know where.

— *Tencer and Cardoso*

Part Three

Three

The next 10%

Chapter 15

Shaping your future

*Every act of creation is first of all
an act of destruction.*

Pablo Picasso (1881-1973) Spanish painter, sculptor

Strategy is essential, but it is the thinking that creates strategies that sits at the core of how a business shapes its future. Time and again, I meet with experienced, senior management who talk in terms of strategy being something that is calculated from a bunch of information and data. Not true. Great strategies are fashioned from creative thinking, not deduced with logical thinking. Daniel Pink, in his book, *A Whole New Mind,* states, "The future belongs to a different kind of person with a different kind of mind ... creative and emphatic 'right-brain' thinkers whose abilities mark the fault line between who gets ahead and who doesn't.[4]" I don't accept Pink's idea that it has to be a "different kind of person;" I believe it can be a different kind of thinking by many of the same people. It's how you think that counts, not who does the thinking. As thought-leaders like Edward De Bono[5] and Howard Gardner[6] say, we are all—well, most of us—capable of creative thinking.

Roger Martin, Dean of the Rotman School of Management at the University of Toronto, makes the point, "In a generative thinking process all strategic-thinking activities are oriented towards creating instead of calculating—inventing instead of finding ... Strategists must leave the intellectual safety of generally accepted concepts to explore new ideas guided by little else than their intuition."[7] Sounds like the first step of entrepreneurial thinking to me.

This and that

I happened to be reading Roger Martin's book, *The Opposable Mind* at the same time that I was delivering a *90% Rule* seminar. During the course of the seminar, we delved into our usual discussion about the potential benefits that the client could offer to their customer base. One participant said, "We can't do both, we have to choose between 'this' or 'that.'"

That got me thinking about Martin's discussion about the pitfalls of "either or" decision-making.

Two little words and a world of difference

I have never thought in terms of "this" **or** "that." To me it is "and." As an entrepreneur, I don't think in terms of "either or," I automatically focus on "this" **and** "that." And then I look for a way to achieve both, collaborate on both or merge both into a whole new idea. What a difference a word can make—"and" or "or." I wholeheartedly subscribe to the idea that thinking in terms of "and" rather than "or" can be mind-changing, especially for a company that needs more innovative thinking.

The challenge is to develop a pragmatic means to demonstrate, to a wide range of your people (not just CEOs and senior management), how to approach "this" *and* "that"

4 *A Whole New Mind*, Daniel H. Pink, Riverhead Books/Penguin, 2005
5 *Six Thinking Hats* by Edward De Bono, Little, Brown and Company, 1999
6 *Leading Minds* by Howard Gardner, Harper Collins Publishers, 1995
7 *The Opposable Mind*, Roger Martin, Harvard Business School Press, 2007

The challenge is to develop a pragmatic means to demonstrate, to a wide range of your people (not just CEOs and senior management), how to approach "this" *and* "that" thinking. The solution lies in something that I have been using for years, the Venn Diagram.

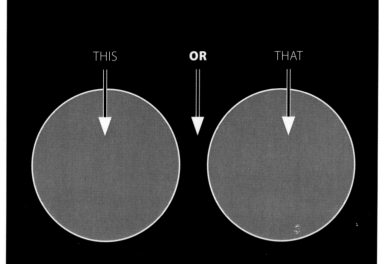

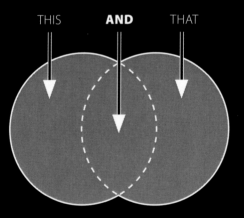

thinking. The solution lies in something that I have been using for years, the Venn Diagram.

Let's call one circle of the Venn Diagram "this" and the other one "that." What I want to identify is the point at which they intersect because this is the common ground that demonstrates "and" *exists*. The intersecting circles help people to visualize how two seemingly opposing ideas separated by "or" can come together, find common ground and become a whole new idea evolving out of the original two.

From this point on, everybody is discussing the "and." It turns team discussion toward finding ways to increase this point of intersection. What emerges is the realization that there is a different way to see established paradigms and beliefs and it goes a long way to making the new kind of thinking stick. It can be transformative.

Two examples

- **Not-for-profit association:** In a NFP "this *and* that" usually revolve around the battle between the desire to build membership with the need for revenue (which can be built from either member or non-member offers). For argument's sake, let's say, membership is "this" and revenue is "that."

  Let's call the overlap "member benefits." As an association moves to create value through events (that non-members can attend at a premium price) the benefits of membership will be better understood and valued by non-members, and the conversion rate to membership will increase. Ultimately, membership and revenue become the same opportunity.

- **Spyder Works:** We used to see "this" as referring to revenue derived from one-to-one (consulting) engagements and "that" as referring to revenue derived from one-to-many opportunities (seminars, books, articles, speaking). In the past we defined our business by how we would engage people. Then we realized that there was a point of intersection between one-to-one and one-to-many and that was our intellectual property—the knowledge that we gain and share. The realization is that the intellectual property, not the delivery system, was the primary driver of our business.

Today, everything we do begins with the discussion about the development of thought-leading intellectual property. How and with whom we disseminate or share it follows.

Joseph Schumpeter in his work, *Capitalism, Socialism and Democracy*, developed the concept of creative destruction to define a "process of industrial mutation that incessantly revolutionizes the economic structure from within, incessantly destroying the old one, incessantly creating a new one."[8] In essence, Schumpeter was talking about innovation and entrepreneurship and redefining "what is" by replacing it with "what could be."

Admittedly, it's not an easy concept to get more than a handful of people to embrace. Not everyone is comfortable with giving up "this" to get to "that." And it takes time for some people to develop their entrepreneurial thinking. But try applying the Venn Diagram next time you are struggling to bring collective new thinking to the table.

The intersection of these two circles is a big part of the *90% Rule* process and it is where the future begins to take shape. It's where divergent thinking (a.k.a. brainstorming, lateral thinking, out-of-the-box thinking, disruptive thinking, audacity) explores the possibilities, contemplates what can be

[8] Joseph Schumpeter, *Creating Modern Capitalism*, Thomas McGraw, p. 2, Harvard Press,

and then—and only then—begins the convergent thinking that funnels the many into the few, the creative into the innovative and converts them into actionable opportunities.

"And" not "or."

— *Tencer and Cardoso*

Chapter 16

Making a decision

Simplicity is an indispensable element of a leader's most important function.

Jack Welch, former CEO, General Electric

A good quick question to ask yourself before you jump into something—a gut check—can be: "Is it yummy or is it yucky?" Let me explain.

As a young entrepreneur, I was stalled in trying to make a business decision relating to the growth of my business. At dinner one night with a successful, self-made businessman, I asked his advice. I was expecting something that, on its cover at least, was a little more sage than what I got. But what I got has stuck with me for years. He picked up the sugar bowl in one hand and the saltshaker in the other. He said, "I want you to make a gut decision." And he asked, "Is the opportunity yummy or yucky?"

I find some of the most brilliant breakthroughs are the simplest ones, insights that most of us miss. It's not because we're not smart enough, it's just that we are too involved and

I find some of the most brilliant breakthroughs are the simplest ones, insights that most of us miss. It's not because we're not smart enough, it's just that we are too involved and always tend to see only the complexity in those things that we are too close to. We don't step back and see the complexity from a higher, more comprehensive and clearer level.

always tend to see only the complexity in those things that we are too close to. We don't step back and see the complexity from a higher, more comprehensive and clearer level.

When we do have a systematic means for relating tactical decisions to broad visionary thinking, what might appear to be a gut decision based on a hunch is actually grounded in what we at Spyder Works call an "Intellectual Gut Check.™" This is when you connect what you intellectually already understand of the current situation (you know that despite looking similar, salt and sugar are different) with a broad gut understanding that you have systematically developed over time. You choose the sugar over the salt based on previously developed information—indispensable elements—that is inherent in your thought process. The decision seems like a simple gut check, and "yummy" is obvious.

The *90% Rule* is grounded in this principle of developing an ingrained process and building a cumulative body of thought, throughout the organization, that minimizes guesswork and eliminates unfounded gut decisions while encouraging and supporting well-founded gut decisions.

The culmination of this disciplined and soul-searching process—all the thinking, questioning, prodding, researching and sharing of the Advil®—now comes together, with the gut and intellect of many working closely as entrepreneurial partners—innovation.

Pass the sugar, please.

Make a decision that is grounded in experience, thoughtfulness and process. There are no guarantees but it makes more sense than throwing darts blindfolded.

— *Tencer and Cardoso*

Chapter 17

Growing your own

One of my favorite advertisements was an early one for the American Express Gold Card. The headline, "Nobody ever promised you a rose garden, so you grew your own." It resonated with me as a young business student and aspiring entrepreneur, and has since stuck with me for decades. It is a constant reminder for me of the principle that life makes no promises, but offers plenty of opportunities. In fact, the process set out in this book grew out of my continuing search for better and better ways to uncover more and more of the opportunities that life presents.

I hope that it has already caused you to examine, question, change and apply new thinking to the way you think about your business. And that through the implementation of the principles and steps, it will enable you to see your business and its intrinsic opportunities more clearly and apply the leverage power of the *90% Rule.*

As always, I like to end where I began and remind you of the three fundamentals that underlie everything that we have worked through.

1) How to foster continuous innovation and growth through the doctrine of entrepreneurial thinking— "innovation against all odds"—by leveraging intellectual and customer capital, continually generating ideas and opportunities and executing it all without bundles of additional money.

2) How to develop a disciplined process that builds on and reinforces, the best in your organization, people, products and services. And through the principles of entrepreneurial thinking, elevates everything to new levels.

3) How to install and implement a systematic and iterative process that pursues opportunities that you are already 90% capable of achieving.

One last closing thought. Above all, success is about doing, not just talking. Good luck and remember, you are already 90% of the way there.

**Above all,
success is about doing,
not just talking.
Good luck
and remember,
you are already 90%
of the way there.**

AfterWord

About the authors
Acknowledgements

KEN TENCER is Chief Executive Officer of Spyder Works Inc. and a successful entrepreneur who has built international companies spanning manufacturing, product development, distribution and professional services. The key to Ken's success: bringing great innovative thinking to the table—plus over twenty years of "getting it done." Ken considers one of the best compliments he ever received was when a client said, "What I like about you is that there's no fluff."

As co-author and developer of *The 90% Rule* (both the book and collaborative seminar), Ken gets businesses on the right growth track. "What makes businesses successful? Knowing which opportunities to pursue. Our years of hands-on research has proven that the greatest opportunities lie in focusing on those opportunities you are already 90% capable of achieving."

As CEO of Spyder Works, he has helped numerous businesses and not-for-profit corporations create more effective growth plans by focusing on what they do best. Prior to taking the lead at Spyder Works, Ken co-founded and grew Nettlewoods Inc., a manufacturer of private label bath and body care products from its genesis to international firm. Ken's credentials also include working for and successfully growing the businesses of other niche manufacturers and retailers. He began his career with a series of marketing, advertising and communications firms, developing campaigns for a variety of financial service companies, consumer goods manufacturers, retailers and social causes.

He currently sits on the advisory committee of an emerging technology firm, has been the President of a charitable organization and holds both a Bachelor of Commerce with Honors from Carleton University and a Masters of Science in International Management from Boston University (Brussels, Belgium).

JOHN PAULO CARDOSO is Chief Creative Officer of Spyder Works Inc. and a world-class creative director who believes that true design brings meaning to the mass of unrelated needs, wants, ideas and perceptions. John says, "Design thinking is at the core of making sense of everything, from the complexity of overabundance to the simplicity of oneness."

John is responsible for ensuring that creativity, in all its forms, through all the firm's work, manifests itself in business results. As John says, "Creativity represents the emotional elements of every experience, but if it does not move the business, what's the point of the experience."

With over twenty years in design, John has brought his unconventional thinking to clients in many industries, from emerging businesses to multinational corporations developing packaging, brands and corporate identities.

John founded Spyder Desktop Studio in 1992 to support the development of leading international brands such as Agfa, Estée Lauder and Revlon. In 2003, he formed Spyder Works Inc. with Ken, transforming the firm from a leading provider of creative design to a comprehensive provider of business and marketing strategy, integrated design and communications.

At Spyder Works John leads the creative team with innovative branding models including the Triad of Retail Brand Development™, Content Enhancement™ and Visual Echo™. John is also the co-developer of the firm's model for integrated business and design thinking, Building Business by Design®.

John has an Honors BA in Fine Art History from the University of Toronto and holds a certificate of design from the internationally acclaimed Art Centre in Toronto.

Acknowledgements

The *90% Rule* is the culmination of many years of hands-on research, practical experience and the innate inspiration we both acquired growing up in entrepreneurial families. When we co-founded our strategic consultancy, we were convinced of the benefits of combining creative and pragmatic thinking into an integrated process. We knew there was a "better way" and, at the time, our favorite anecdote was from the early space program—how the Americans spent millions of dollars developing a pen that would work in space while the Russians simply used a pencil. When creativity and logic are fused you get innovation—and simplicity. We wanted to build something that would demystify and simplify the integration of business strategy and design thinking, as well as give companies a pragmatic and systematic means of actually achieving it. This book is an acknowledgement of having reached an important milestone on that journey.

Like it takes a village to raise a child, it takes a group of people to nurture, shape and write a book. From its conception to the final manuscript, we are grateful to all who have supported and helped us along the way. We thank Nicolas Papadopoulos who explained to Ken that, while a book must center around a focused idea, the sum of words is comparable to the number of e-mails and reports that he wrote in a short span of time. This inspired Ken to begin—to lock himself in a hotel room for a long weekend to write the first ten thousand words.

Thanks to our friends and colleagues Leslie Hayman, Allan Lever, Lori Freeman, Eric Klein, Susan Rosenthal and Warren Blatt who recognized and supported our somewhat different and "refreshing" approach to business. And thanks to Rick Spence, Norm Oulster and Cathy Carter who pushed us to write a book about our thinking and the process. As well, our trusted advisors, who have been a guide and sounding-board: Marion Plunkett, Philip Mendes da Costa, Roy Sieben, Adrian Davis, Katherine Van de Mark, Elaine Holding and Esther Mamane. Also, to Tom Gattis, Robert Fee and Victor Ermoli who recognized that our process had application within an academic setting. Last but not least, we would like to thank David Hughes. Without his encouragement, advice, perseverance, insight and special talent this book would not have come to fruition. Thank you David.

Also, we thank others who played an essential role in framing our work around projects that offered an exploration into the *90% Rule*—all our clients who never stop inspiring us to great heights and gave us crucial feedback: Peter Hohman, Beverly Topping, Wayne Parent, Chris Gale, Vicki Jordan, Yahya Abbas, Marlene Novack, Ted Hellyer, Carey-Ann Oestreicher, Fred Stewart, Nathan Helder, Robert Koss, Jenny Longo, Dawna Matton, Margaret Parent, Erica Carr, Ian Hancock, Christian Buhagiar, Jennifer Mulholland, George Horich and Pat Diamond. And of course, to the inventor of the alarm clock for helping us through all the early morning wake-ups after late night edits.

A final thank you to those who are closest and dearest to us, our families. They're the ones that have put up with our midnight crawls to our laptops, early morning getups and extended absences. A special thank you to Laura, Tommy and Sofia. Thank you to Elizabeth Cardoso for being everything that I cannot be and who manages the lives of three very busy boys Noah, Nathaniel and Quinn. Lastly, we thank our parents David Tencer, Glenys Tencer, Manuel Pinto Cardoso, and Concieção Cardoso.

Ken Tencer and John Paulo Cardoso